I0210614

Fr♥m Me
to Us

4 Steps *from* Single *to* Married Life

April Crimbley

Copyright © 2019 by April Crimbley

All rights reserved. No part of this book may be used or reproduced by any means, graphic, electronic, or mechanical, including photo-copying, recording, taping or by any information storage retrieval system without the written permission of the publisher except in the case of brief quotations embodied in critical articles and reviews.

Because of the dynamic nature of the Internet, any Web addresses or links contained in this book may have changed since publication and may no longer be valid.

All scripture quotations, unless otherwise indicated, are taken from the HOLY BIBLE, NEW INTERNATIONAL VERSION®. NIV® Copyright © 1973, 1978, 1984 by International Bible Society. Used by permission of Zondervan Publishing House. All rights reserved.

The "NIV" and "New International Version" trademarks are regis-tered in the United States Patent and Trademark Office by Interna-tional Bible Society. Use of either trademark requires the permission of the International Bible Society.

Design and Layout by Michael Grossman
www.mg-grafik.com

Editing by Michelle Chester
www.ebm-services.com

ISBN: 978-1-7334011-0-4 (pbk)
ISBN: 978-1-7334011-1-1 (ebk)

Printed in the United States of America

Also by April Crimbley

Single Dose: Finding Peace, Fulfillment, and Contentment Being Single

Listed as author, April Harding
ISBN: 978-1-7334011-9-7

For My Husband

I dedicate this book to my husband who accepts and loves me for who I am and motivates me to pursue my goals until I accomplish them. Thank you for opening your heart and allowing me to get to know and love you. I'm so grateful to get to grow in lifelong intimacy with you.

Contents

♡

Introduction

When I got married in 2009, I was so excited to know that I would be spending the rest of my life with someone I truly love. The desire to meet someone to share my hopes and dreams with for a lifetime was finally coming true. I was divorced for years and had actually settled into being single. I resolved within myself that I did not want to remarry and that if I did, I would probably never meet anyone. I was enjoying being single and had established a pretty good life structure and was enjoying my daily routines. I learned so much about how to manage the challenges of single life that I published a book titled *Single Dose: Finding Peace, Fulfillment, and Contentment Being Single.* I loved the freedom of being able to choose meals, movies, and how I spent my time without having to consider a spouse. I loved the quietness and stillness of my home and so many other things about being single.

Well, fast forward eleven years after publishing *Single Dose* and here I am married again. To my pleasant surprise, I met someone who met almost everything I wanted in a husband. Married life has been wonderful; however, I was so used to being single that it took me a while to adjust to being married again. For the most part, it was a smooth transition moving from single to married, but I did find myself struggling with a few things. I was quickly reminded that when you are forming a new life with someone, it takes time to adjust. One of the things that I had to adjust to was learning how to share my physical space at home. Basic things like less closet space took effort to adjust to.

Fortunately, my husband and I have a lot of the same values regarding religion, housekeeping, intimacy, finances, and other areas. We were able to merge our lives pretty smoothly. In other areas though, there were individual challenges that took longer for both of us to overcome. Transitioning from being single and independent to merging your life with someone else's is exciting yet tricky even when you are deeply in love and seriously committed to each other. Even when we have the same hopes and dreams of married life, we still may not have the capability of successfully managing differences. It took a few years for us to comfortably merge our single habits and routines into a productive married lifestyle that we both enjoy.

It's so exciting to meet that special person and decide to spend the rest of your life with him/her. Once the decision is made, a wedding date is set and you eventually get married. You might have a huge wedding with a big bridal party and over 300 guests. You might decide to have a destination wedding in Jamaica or some other island. You might have a small wedding at a church with family and a few close friends. You might keep it simple and save money by pledging your vows before a judge at the local municipal court. **How you plan to celebrate your wedding vows is not as important as how you prepare for this lifelong celebration of love.**

Marriage is something that you should commit to for a lifetime. You should sincerely and seriously pledge your loyalty to the person you are marrying. There should be no turning back once you sign that marriage certificate and say your wedding vows.

I would like to share with you what I have learned about loyalty, commitment, and love as I shifted from single to married life. My personal experiences and mistakes, in addition to years of research and observation of other couples, have been valuable to me. The transition to married life is fun and exciting, and it can also be challenging as you get to know each other.

From Me to Us offers a roadmap for making your shift from single to married life a smooth one.

How to Use this Book

From Me to Us provides instructions and practical advice for those who are trying to figure out how to transition their productive and fulfilling single life into married life that will be just as fulfilling or more. Each chapter includes specific steps and also questions for personal reflection to help cement what you learn. It might also be a good idea to discuss some of the things you learn with your spouse or spouse-to-be. It's important to note though, that From Me to Us is for you to evaluate your personal mindset regarding marriage.

This is not a dating book or a marriage book. It's not even a premarital counseling book. It is a book that will prepare you as an individual to walk into your marriage with a greater sense of who you are taking into the marriage. From Me to Us will also set you on a journey to get to know your future spouse better. Knowing this will help you enter into the marriage with a greater sense of love, purpose, and wholeness.

There is no one size fits all. What works for one person or couple may not work for another person or couple. As you read this book, use the information that works for you.

From Me to Us will prepare you for a lifelong celebration of love by presenting some things for you to think about and consider. When you return from the honeymoon or the wedding ceremony, there's a certain mind shift that needs to take place to move from being single to married. This book will present those areas you need to think about as you transition into marriage.

From Me to Us is for men and women, young and older people who are engaged to be married. It's also for those who are remarrying or who have never been married. If you are already married, you can use this book to start over in your relationship. Single people can also use this book to think about what to look for in a relationship.

The Bible is an important part of my life and has been the spiritual foundation for the decisions I make for my life. Because I feel that the Bible is essential in marital success when both parties participate, I have listed relevant scriptures at the end of each chapter. The scripture will serve as a foundation or a "why" for each step.

My hope and prayer are that, as you read *From Me to Us*, your heart will be open to taking the steps necessary to grow from a single life of peace, fulfillment, and contentment to a marriage of solidarity, love, and happiness.

The chapters (steps) in this book form a circle that leads you back to the first step in the process. This creates a way for you to revisit the steps for continuous growth.

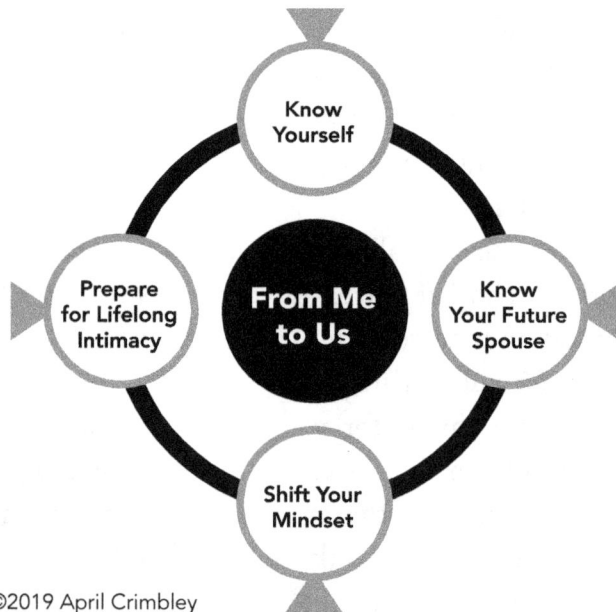

Know Yourself

Prepare for Lifelong Intimacy

From Me to Us

Know Your Future Spouse

Shift Your Mindset

©2019 April Crimbley

10 Reasons It's
Great to be Married

In my first book, *Single Dose: Finding Peace, Fulfillment, and Contentment Being Single*, I listed ten reasons it's great to be single. Sometimes life gets so busy that we don't take time to focus on the important things. Lists tend to take our memory back to those important things. Here's a list of ten reasons it's great to be married. Bookmark this page and read the list often to remind yourself of some of the many reasons why you got married.

1. You get to grow old with the person you love and love spending time with.

2. You have someone you can share and trust your innermost private thoughts with.

3. You have an automatic date every day of your life.

4. You have a partner to attain goals, plan travel, and spend holidays with.

5. You have someone to help you make decisions.

6. You'll have more sex. Married people have sex more regularly than single people.

7. You'll have more passionate intimacy because you have a deeper and more committed relationship.

8. Cold nights are warmer and cozier with the person you love.

9. You'll have more financial security because you manage your money with each other in mind.

10. You have someone with whom to share the household chores.

Chapter One

♡

Take Time to Get to Know Yourself

The first step in moving from single to married life is to know who you are.

I t's ironic to say this, but you have to have a strong sense and belief in yourself before you can believe in the person you are going to marry. It takes a certain level of strength and confidence just to make it in this world. To be able to believe in yourself, you have to know who you are. Knowing who you are and what makes you "tick" is critical to your preparation for marriage. When you know who you are and how to love and be kind to yourself, you'll be able to show love and kindness to your spouse. Knowing who you are will help you identify the type of relationship you should or should *not* be in. If you don't know yourself, how will you know what type of person you should be with?

In marriage, it should be two independently content people merging their personalities into one healthy relationship. You should not depend on marriage to make you complete. You should already have a sense of contentment in your life when you get married. **It would be a huge and unfair responsibility for your spouse to have to try and make you happy, if you're not already happy.**

Hopefully, the person you marry will make you feel more secure and bring more joy into your life; however, the keyword here is "more." You should already have fulfillment in your life as a single person. Then, when the two of you come together in marriage, you will bring more security, pleasure, thrill, and pure joy into each other's lives. When you are complete before marriage, you will be even more complete after marriage.

To find out if you really know yourself, take time to look at yourself and think about who you are. Spend time alone and get to know you. If you have recently left a relationship, spend time alone before you go into another relationship. Sometimes we can get so caught up in a relationship that we forget who we are. When you leave a relationship, you need time to figure out who you are before you share your time with someone else. Form your own routines and learn your own likes and dislikes. If you are currently living with your parents, children, or a roommate, find somewhere to spend time alone and get to know you. You can visit somewhere quiet like a local park or library. Take into consideration things like:

- *What makes me happy? How do I act or react when I'm happy?*
- *What makes me sad? How do I act or react when I'm sad?*
- *What makes me angry? How do I act or react when I'm angry?*
- *When do I most feel like myself?*
- *What's the first thing I want to do when I have some free time?*

Knowing how to be comfortable with yourself will help you to be a more mature person. If you're not sure who you are, spend time getting to know yourself. As you spend time alone, you'll learn more about the things you like and dislike. You'll know your preferences and desires. This will help you when you need to make decisions.

Our past relationships and friendships can help us understand ourselves. Think about the times in the past when you became angry and reacted out of that anger. What happened to cause that? This will give you an idea of the things that "trigger" the emotions of anger.

Think about times in your life when you laughed out loud or just felt incredibly happy. What was happening during that time? This will give you an idea of the types of things you enjoy doing.

Look through old photo albums for an idea of your personality. Look at your clothes, the books you read, and other cherished possessions you have in your home. What items remind you of your true personality?

Sometimes the comments that people make about us can shed light on the image we are presenting to them. That image may not be the same way we think we are. But it is something to consider since this is what you are demonstrating based on their perception. If you have heard more than two or three people give you a particular compliment, it's worth taking into consideration. I'm not talking about the generic statement, "you are beautiful" or "you are nice." I'm talking about specific compliments people have given you. Perhaps someone has told you that you're smart, organized, a great cook, giving, straight-forward, bubbly, good with your hands, a people-person. If more than two or three people have told you the same thing, it just might be true. Don't minimize the value of any of the compliments you receive.

On the flip side, there are people in this world who are cynical and tend to see the negative side of everything and everybody. They can look at a beautiful sunflower and call it a weed. People like this are usually speaking from their own negative perception of life. I'm not sure why, but some people just tend to think negatively about everything. If you've had the unfortunate experience of living with someone like this in your family, take time to get rid of all the negative things they've ever said about you. Replace those negative comments about you with positive affirmations while at the same time being aware of your weaknesses. Work to strengthen your weak areas, but at the same time, focus on your strengths in order to maintain healthy self-esteem.

Knowing yourself will be important as you move into married life. As you get to know yourself, you'll have a better grip of who you are presenting to your spouse. You'll know what your tastes and preferences are as you share your life with him/her.

Here are some ways to spend time getting to know you:

- Take time alone, away from work, people, or any obligations. Just sit and think about who you are.

- Treat yourself to dinner or a movie alone. This will help you to be comfortable sharing your time with just yourself.

- Get a journal and pour your heart out on paper. If there are deep secrets that you can't talk to anyone about, write them in your journal. Writing your thoughts, fears, and worries can be healing to your heart. A journal will allow you to release thoughts and concerns that you can't share with anyone else. Sometimes, if I'm struggling with something, I'll write a letter in my journal as if I'm writing to a counselor. Then I'll read the letter as if I am the counselor and write a response. I've resolved a lot of situations this way and feel much better after.

- Read through old journals you've kept in the past. You can get an idea of how you think and respond in situations. You'll also be able to see how you have grown.

- Look at old photos to get an idea of your personality.

When you know yourself, you are able to proclaim something like, "I'm a person who loves to laugh and have fun." "I don't like being around people." "I love to feel needed by my family and friends." "I love to shop. Shopping makes me happy." "I'm a night owl and love staying up late every night." "I love to travel and meet new people." "I'm a very spiritual person." These are just examples of statements you should be able to make once you discover who you really are.

Know Your Personality

Knowing yourself involves knowing your personality. What is your true personality? It's very important that you allow it to show.

When you are authentic in your interactions with people, they will be able to see who you really are. When you show your true self, your spouse will know who he/she is marrying. **Marriage is a lifelong journey which is a long time to pretend to be someone you are not.** To avoid having to pretend, start getting to know your true personality.

Imagine you are sitting alone in a room. The room is quiet. You have nowhere to go and nothing to do. You have all day to do whatever you want to do. What are you thinking at this very moment? What would you like to do? Whatever you are thinking is a good indication of the type of personality you have. If you desire to go out and do something with friends, that's a good sign that you love being around people. Are you thinking you would love to cuddle up on the couch with a good book or watch television alone? That's a good sign that you are a loner. I believe we all have different preferences at different times in our lives. Think about what you prefer most of the time—a quiet day alone or an active day with friends or family.

Focus on being yourself rather than trying to be the person you think your spouse wants you to be. Don't try to be the wife or husband you see in other relationships. You never know what goes on behind closed doors in other marriages. Sometimes marriages look great to others watching; but if you spend time in that home and watch their interaction with each other, you'll notice they're not as loving with each other as they seemed. I've observed couples that seem to be a solid couple, but after spending time with them, there was not only a lack of affection between them but there was also discord. Your goal in your marriage should be to be the best couple you can be for each other. Don't try to be like any other couple. Your relationship is unique just as the two of you are unique.

Hopefully you feel comfortable being yourself when you are with the person you are marrying. Your life will be more joyful if you are able to express your authenticity. I knew a woman once who had to suppress her smile and friendliness whenever she went out with her husband. Because of his jealousy and insecurities, he would become angry if she smiled at or spoke to anyone. This caused her true personality to be stunted and she eventually went into a miserable shell. Her friendliness and his jealousy are things they should have discovered before marriage.

If your fiancé is an insecure person who is not very friendly, and you are outgoing and friendly with everyone, it could cause problems. In this type of marriage, the two individuals will have to learn how to modify their interactions with others so that the other person is not uncomfortable.

Start expressing the true "you" to make sure your spouse is comfortable with that. Ask yourself:

- *What is my personality? Am I bubbly, talkative, or am I quiet and shy?*
- *Do I like to have fun, or am I the more serious type?*
- *Am I outgoing and love to talk to friends and even people I don't know, or am I kind of reserved?*
- *Is my future spouse comfortable with my personality, or does he/she ask me to change how I act at times?*

You will be more interesting to your spouse as you walk in your own personality. Nobody wants to be married to a robot. Robots are man-made and are programmed to perform certain activities. You are a live human being created by God. You have feelings, intellect, dreams, and desires. Know yourself so that you'll know what you are bringing into the relationship. When you know yourself and love yourself, you'll be able to love someone else freely also. When you love yourself, you know how you want to feel and be in your next relationship.

Know Your Style

Knowing yourself not only means knowing your personality but it also means knowing your personal style. Style involves the way you dress, walk, wear your hair, and how you carry yourself. Your style is how you present yourself to the world or the people in your circle. It's what distinguishes you from other people. Your style is your authentic you. Your style is not only how you see yourself but also how others see you. It's about what you contribute to those around you.

To help identify your style, ask yourself:

- *Who is the "authentic" me?*
- *How do I present myself to the world or those around me?*
- *What are my qualities and attributes?*
- *What image do I want to present to those around me?*
- *Am I conservative or traditional in how I dress, or do I dress trendy?*

How to Establish Your Personal Style

1. List three adjectives that describe your personality. Be honest and true to who you are.

2. Once you identify your personal style, write it down in a journal or keep it close to your heart.

3. Plant the vision of yourself in your mind. Focus on the strengths that God gave you and don't downplay them. To downplay your true self is to downplay your Creator. There's a reason you are here in this world and that you have the personality that you do. If you suppress your personality and your true identity, you are not fulfilling your purpose, even if you don't know what your purpose is.

4. Be aware of your personal style every time you step out the door. Think about the words you use, how you dress, and the actions you take at work and everywhere you go. Ask yourself if your words and actions align with your personal style.

5.   Don't ever lose who you are. Always be yourself. Why? Because there is no one in this world like you. And you should never try to be like anyone else. If you try to be like someone else, you are not fulfilling the space that was designed for you.

You may feel that you are not as strong or as good in some areas as someone else is. That's okay. Focus on your own strengths and what you are good at. Comparison only creates insecurities in our minds. Don't ever compare yourself to someone else. There will always be someone stronger, bigger, and better. Instead of comparing yourself to others, compare yourself to your best vision of yourself. Then strive to reach that vision.

Being yourself takes courage. There's so much peer pressure to be like the images we see on television. Own your personality and walk completely in it day after day. Don't hide who you are. Complete the space that's made for you and share yourself with the world.

Know Your Life Purpose

A part of knowing yourself is pursuing your life purpose. Knowing your life purpose is a pursuit that some accomplish full blast and others seek their entire lives. I believe we were all created on this earth for a reason. And that reason usually involves helping others in some capacity whether directly or indirectly. There's a space in this world that only your individual personality can fill. We each have a purpose in life. We each have a unique personality. Even though some people go through their entire life not knowing what their purpose or calling is, one thing is for sure, there is no one else on this earth like you or like me.

A purpose is "the reason for which something is done or created or for which something exists." It could also be called a "calling," "gift," or "talent." Just the fact that we exist in this life means that we have a purpose. Your purpose is not for you, it's for others around you.

For some people, their purpose is found in the work they do. For some people, it's in their gifts and talents like singing or painting. Purpose is about recognizing your own contribution to the world whether it's in the work you do, playing music, helping friends, or bringing joy into the lives of those around you. A purpose isn't necessarily something grandiose or something that puts you in the public eye. Sometimes it's the smaller things that can make a huge impact on someone's life. Your purpose could be something as simple yet impactful as always having a warm smile. A smile makes a huge impact in people's lives. Smiles are contagious. With all the turmoil in the world that happens on a daily basis, a smile can make a huge difference in someone's life. If you are a person who tends to naturally smile a lot, don't suppress it. The world needs your smile.

Here are some examples that some have stated is their life purpose.

- Spread the gospel of Jesus Christ to the world.

- Work with my hands to make things or fix things.

- Play music.

- Help single parents with managing life.

- Work with children.

- Be a nurse and help people who are in pain.

- Help people discover their purpose.

- Organize things.

To realize your purpose doesn't mean you will be hit by a huge beam of light or sent into a trance. Realizing your purpose happens when you recognize that your actions, personality, and desires align with your heart's compassion regarding a specific thing. That realization can come when you are doing something that makes you feel fulfilled. **More than likely, your purpose in life is something you are already doing but just don't realize it yet.**

I recognized my purpose pretty late in life—around age 37, although I had been serving in my purpose all my life and didn't know it. The day I realized my purpose, I was teaching Sunday School in church. A strong sense of fulfillment came over me. It felt like a strong and sweet presence was completely surrounding me. The feeling was so powerful that I cried tears of joy and wonder. It felt like God Himself was there saying, *Yes! This is why I created you—to teach!* I felt the same "stirring" whenever I conducted training, wrote inspirational messages, and even read and learned something new. A sense of validation continuously overwhelms me when I teach in any capacity or learn something new.

Once I realized my purpose, I recalled my childhood when I wrote plays, poems, and stories and recognized that I was being pulled into my destiny all along. I thought about being asked to teach life skills classes at work and Sunday School classes at church at age 24. The people who asked me to teach saw something in me that aligned with my purpose in life. And because I said "yes," I was propelled into the journey to fulfill my purpose.

What I'm trying to say is that your purpose could be hidden in something until you start working in it. When you try something new that you're drawn to, or you answer someone's call to lead something or volunteer, your purpose will be revealed to you.

Think back over your life and ask yourself, *What are some activities I've participated in that made me feel fulfilled? What have I done in the past or who have I helped that made me feel elevated afterwards?* What's in your heart that is pulling you to do something? It could be work or volunteering, or it could be a certain type of person that you always seem to encounter who needs your help. Who is that person that you always come in contact with and end up helping? What have you been complimented on repeatedly for doing something in particular? Maybe that's the reason you're here on this earth.

I have a dear friend who called me early one Saturday morning with some exciting news. She called to tell me she finally found her purpose in life. I asked her to tell me what happened to help her realize her purpose. She said she attended a women's conference the night before and the speaker asked the audience some questions about their purpose. The questions helped her realize that she was already fulfilling her purpose, which is to help young ladies in need. She thought back over her life and how it seemed that she always tended to encounter young ladies who either needed a ride, a babysitter, or advice. She always seemed to be in places where she met this type of person. Her purpose was confirmed in her heart at the conference.

I'm pretty certain that this is the case with most people—you are already fulfilling your purpose without even realizing what it is. Don't stress yourself if you are unsure of what your life purpose is. Just rest assure that you are important to this universe. The fact that you are living and breathing means that your existence matters and that you have an opportunity to make this world a better place.

Pursuing your purpose might be a lifelong journey. It's okay if it takes a lifetime to pursue it. There's no need to rush. The important thing to remember is to enjoy the journey. Whether you are pursuing your purpose or confirming it, allow your purpose to be your guide as you make decisions in life. The choices you make in life should be in line with your purpose. Whenever you are approached with a difficult decision, ask yourself, *How does this align with my life purpose?*

Knowing that you are important is critical as you move into married life. Seeing your value and place in this world will help create a sense of fulfillment that you will take into your marriage. That confidence will pour over into your affection and feelings for your spouse. It will also help you stand tall during the tough times in your marriage. It will give you the confidence you need to withstand the difficult times. At times, problems and challenges in life may overwhelm you, but if you know you have a purpose and a reason for living, it will help you to carry on.

How to Discover Your Life Purpose

1. Think back to your childhood, teen, and young adult years and ask yourself, *What have I always been drawn to?*

2. Ask yourself what type of work you would love to do if you could do anything you wanted to do and could start tomorrow. This will reveal where your heart is.

3. Think about what you enjoy doing in your spare time—work with your hands, design clothes, write songs, read, volunteer with children, work with the elderly, take care of sick people. This will reveal what you have a passion for.

4. Ask yourself what types of people you have compassion for when you see them— children, homeless, elderly, prisoners, disabled, veterans. This is a clue of your purpose in life because your heart is drawn toward them. When your heart is in what you do, it provides the energy you need to press forward when times get hard.

5. Start taking steps now to try new things. Volunteer with those groups you're drawn to. Your purpose will eventually become clear to you as you explore those activities or people you serve or work with.

Know Your Goals and Dreams

Knowing yourself involves knowing what your personal goals and dreams are. Single people have dreams about their lives, but they have only their needs (and their children's needs if they have children) to consider as they make plans to accomplish them.

Most of the time those dreams are about careers, financial accomplishments, or traveling. For a lot of women and some men, they wonder about having a family with children. As a single moving into marriage, you probably feel that you are moving closer to accomplishing your dreams or you may even feel that you're moving away from them.

Moving into marriage should not put a halt to your desire to accomplish your dreams. Everyone should have goals and dreams. It gives you something to reach for and keeps you motivated. There is a difference between a goal and a dream, though. A goal has a specific timeline with specific dates and it usually has a target finish date. It also helps to write goals down on paper so that you don't forget those specific dates.

A dream is something you imagine that seems kind of remote. It's an ideal situation that almost seems like a fantasy. It's okay to have dreams as long as you are not stagnate waiting for your dreams to come true. It's more productive to work toward your goals since goals are more realistic. Goals can usually be accomplished because resources are within your reach.

Dreams are usually pretty remote and give you something to reach for and look forward to one day. Your dreams may or may not be a reality but there is no harm in dreaming. Dreaming motivates you and energizes you. Think about what your dreams are and what you would like to accomplish one day.

What are your goals? Do you have the resources to make your goals a reality? If not, then they're probably dreams. It's important to know the difference in the two because you'll need to make your decisions on how to access resources to accomplish them. As you think about moving into marriage, you'll want to know which goals and/or dreams you should pursue. **If your goals or dreams won't pay the bills, you'll need to consider how to make alternate income while you pursue your goals.**

Know Your Strengths and Weaknesses

Knowing your strengths and weaknesses is a part of getting to know yourself. Knowing your strengths will help you put your best foot forward in your relationship. For example, if managing money is one of your strengths, you can volunteer to be the household finance manager. The household finance manager is the one who manages the household budget, makes sure the bills are paid on time, and other household financial duties as needed.

Some examples of strengths you might have are:

- Showing loyalty and commitment

- Managing and saving money

- Being dependable when asked to perform a task

- Seeing the good in people

- Finding deals and discounts

- Showing compassion and empathy

- Organizing and planning

- Communicating with people effectively

- Staying positive in negative situations

- Building or fixing things

Knowing your weaknesses will signal you when you need to make adjustments. There might be times when you're in a situation in your marriage when there's a need that you don't have the capacity to fill because of your weakness in that area. These are times when you have to communicate this to your spouse so that adjustments can be made. For example, you might be a procrastinator who is always late. This is something you can share upfront with your spouse so that planning and preparation can be discussed prior to important events.

When situations in your marriage call for your strengths, you will be able to help. When situations in your marriage call for something you know you have a weakness in, don't set yourself up for failure by "signing up" for those activities.

Some examples of weaknesses are:

- Using bad language when you're angry

- Not cleaning your house often because you don't see it as a priority

- Being an impulsive shopper and sometimes spending a lot of money that is not in the budget

- A need to receive compliments from men or women other than your spouse

- An uncontrollable urge to tell lies

- Complaining a lot or being pessimistic

- Overacting to difficult situations and having at times been called a "drama queen"

Start working on those weak areas before you get married so that they don't cause too big of a problem in your marriage. Use your strengths to contribute to the growth of the marriage while at the same time developing your weak areas. Work together with your spouse to figure out how to leverage each of your strengths to build the marriage. Be patient with your spouse in learning his/her weaknesses. Realize that you have weaknesses too, and you want the same patience for your weaknesses.

Know Your Religious Preference

Knowing yourself involves knowing your religious preference—whether you want religion to play a part in your life or not. "Religion" is defined as the belief in God, a god, or in a group of gods; an organized system of beliefs, ceremonies, and rules used to worship God, a god, or a group of gods; an interest, a belief, or an activity that is very important to a person or group. "Religious" is defined as relating to or manifesting faithful devotion to an acknowledged ultimate reality or deity; Of, relating to, or devoted to religious beliefs or observances as part of a religious order. There are hundreds, maybe thousands of religions in the world. Knowing yourself means knowing if you want religion to play a part in your life or not.

Some people identify more with the word "spiritual" instead of "religious." Spiritual is more about faith in God not necessarily affiliated with any organized religion. Spirituality is that part of us that is composed of our personal values and beliefs and provides purpose for our lives. It is the core of who we are. Being spiritual includes a sense of connection to something bigger than ourselves and typically involves searching for the meaning of life. Knowing yourself means knowing if you want to pursue spiritual growth for your life.

I believe that everybody has a sense of yearning and pursuit of God deep within, yet we may not be aware that it is God we long for. My faith in God is a very important part of my life. I believe in the deity of God and that He is the source of my life and strength. Faith in God is also a very important part of my husband's life. Our faith in God and our love for each other has been the foundation and saving grace for our marriage. We have learned (and still learning) how to love each other through the Bible, which we believe is God's Word. If it was not for our belief in God and our seeking Him in good times and difficult times, our marriage may not have lasted. We see ourselves as God's children and because of that we can pray and ask for His help during the difficult times.

We all have weaknesses and those weaknesses show up a lot in marriage. Our belief in God has been a mediator for me and my husband, because through Him we were able to find resources that kept us on track when times were hard. Prayer has kept us focused on something greater than ourselves and has kept us strong. Prayer allows us to request help from God when dealing with difficult situations. Attending church and fellowshipping with other believers has also kept our spirits enlightened to God's Word. For some reason, there's a stronger bond and awareness of our love for each other that happens every time we attend church. Praying together helps us see that God is a part of our marriage.

To decide if religion or spirituality will be part of your life, ask yourself,

- *What part does religion or spirituality play in my life?*
- *Am I actively pursuing more knowledge of God, and how will I continue that pursuit in my marriage?*
- *What level of devotion do I desire to have to God?*
- *How will I carry my devotion to God into my marriage?*

If you do desire to have a relationship with God and participate in religious activities in your marriage, now is the time to start. If you start now, you will already have a religious or spiritual foundation when you enter marriage.

If you choose to pursue God and learn more about living for Him in a religious or spiritual capacity, here are some suggestions.

- Pray and ask God to come into your heart and into your life.

- Establish a devotion time with God which is when you spend time praying or talking to Him each day.

- Set aside some time each day to read verses in the Bible in order to get to know God more. The Bible is a story of redemption—The Old Testament shows us how we could never live for God on our own. The New Testament shows us how God redeemed us from failing to live for Him on our own.

- Find a local Bible-teaching church to learn more about God and to fellowship with others.

As you pursue God through prayer and reading the Bible, your faith will increase, and you will already have the groundwork completed for transitioning your religion or spirituality into your marriage. The groundwork will be something you can share with your spouse and hopefully create a deeply positive bond that will be like no other connection in your relationship.

Know Your Values

Knowing your values is a part of knowing who you are. Values are the things you stand for. They are the things you consider to be most important to you in your life. Family, freedom, honesty, integrity, self-reliance, ability, professionalism, happiness, service, trust… are all examples of values.

Your values will help you to make decisions in your life, so it's important to know what they are. As you stay in tune with your values, you'll be in tune with those things that give your life meaning and purpose. They will also guide your behavior in situations you face in life. To help you identify your values, ask yourself:
- *What do I feel a strong sense of conviction about?*
- *What means the most to me as I interact with people?*
- *What's important to me in my life?*

Moral Values

Knowing what your own moral values are will help you identify if your fiancé holds the same values. Merging your life with someone in marriage means associating your lifestyle and image with that person. If you want a positive lifestyle and want to live a life of integrity, decency, and giving, make sure the person you're marrying wants the same thing.

Ask yourself:
- *What do I value in life?*
- *What positive traits do I want others to see in me?*
- *What character flaws do I have that I need to work on and try to diminish?*

Think about the values you want to see in your marriage. Strive to enhance those values by demonstrating those as much as possible. Everyone has weaknesses or bad habits that surface occasionally. Work on the character flaws you have to make sure you are bringing the best "you" into the marriage. Your marriage should be a representation of the best part of you and the person you are marrying. Work on those things that cause you to slip and fall. If you have a problem with lying, practice telling the truth. The more you practice being honest, the more natural it will become to you. Try hard to keep your word when you make promises so that you are not constantly disappointing people.

If you don't see cleaning house as a priority and you regularly leave your house dirty, set a schedule for cleaning your house once or twice a week. As you follow your schedule, it will eventually become a habit and you'll see how easy it is to keep a clean house. Clean up your act now before you merge your life with someone else's. Some character flaws take time to get rid of but do the best you can.

Everyone has flaws whether big or small. The goal is to know what's important for your peace of mind and the level of integrity you want to demonstrate in your daily life. Knowing your values will help you identify if you and your spouse are on the same page. Having the same values will cause you to be more aligned in the decisions you make together.

Relationship Values

Knowing yourself means knowing the types of people you will allow to be a part of your life. "Relationship" is defined as the way in which two or more people or things are connected. "Friend" is defined as one attached to another by affection or esteem. When moving from single to married life, it's important to define which of your relationships and friendships in your single life will continue into your married life.

The relationships you continue will in one way or another become part of your married life. For that reason, it is critical that you and your spouse are on the same page when it comes to which relationships and friendships you will have. Friends can have either a negative, positive, or neutral effect on your marriage. Be aware of which type of effect your friends have on your marriage. Nourish your positive relationships, but be careful with those relationships that cause problems between you and your spouse.

One area regarding relationships and friends is that of the husband's friend who is a girl or the wife's friend who is a guy. Many people have long term friends like this either from childhood, college, work, or other places. While these friendships are great while you're single, they could cause problems in your marriage. You'll need to know if you and your spouse will continue to have friends of the opposite sex after you get married. This is something that you need to make sure you're on the same page about to make sure there's no confusion later. If you agree that you should not have friends of the opposite sex, make sure to honor that decision by not having secret conversations or visits. To have secret conversations or visits will cause distrust to build in your marriage. Trust is very hard to rebuild once it's destroyed. Be careful not to hurt the integrity in your marriage by engaging with friendships or relationships that you think might be offensive to your spouse.

I know some couples in which the husband has female friends or the wife has male friends and it causes no problems in their marriage. These are friends they attended school with or lived with in the same neighborhood as children. Lifelong friendships should be cherished if they are not a hindrance to your married life. Here are some questions to answer to help determine if you should continue your opposite-sex friendships when you get married:

- Is your mate aware of your opposite-sex friendships? If not, why do you feel the need to keep the friendship a secret?

- Would you behave differently around your friend if your spouse were present? If you would, ask yourself why you don't act the same when your spouse is around.

- Would you feel uncomfortable if your spouse had the same quality of friendship with someone of the opposite sex? If the answer is yes, then imagine how your spouse would feel if they knew about your friendship.

- Do you have a physical and/or emotional attraction to your friend? If there is an attraction, it's not physically or emotionally safe to have this friend because of the risk of activity that could threaten the trust in your marriage.

- Do you and your friend ever exchange highly personal details about your lives or complain about your marriage to each other? If so, then you must realize that discussing personal, especially unfavorable information about your spouse is not appropriate because it violates the privacy of your marriage.

If you and your fiancé decide that it is okay to have friends of the opposite sex when you get married, it's important to have boundaries around those friendships. Boundaries will help prevent causing any confusion in your marriage. Some of those boundaries should be:

- Make sure your spouse knows your friend. Also, be certain your mate is completely comfortable with the type and level of interaction you have with him/her. Conversations with your opposite-sex friend should not be hidden and should not only happen when your spouse is not present.

- Honor your spouse's wishes concerning your friendship—even if it means ending it. If your spouse is uncomfortable with the friendship, show your respect for your spouse by letting the friendship go.

- Develop and consistently nurture a "best friend" relationship with your partner so that you'll be able to talk openly with him/her. When you need to talk to your spouse about something sensitive, tell him/her to put on the "best friend hat" to discuss. That way, you are approaching the topic as friends and not as spouses who might otherwise be hurt by the discussion. Being able to talk to your spouse as a friend should eliminate the need to have an opposite-sex friend.

- Develop and consistently cultivate friendships with your female friends (if you're a woman) or male friends (if you're a man). When you do this, you'll have someone to confide in without the risk of falling into an affair or inappropriate relationship.

- Avoid close opposite-sex friendships if you are struggling in your marriage. When there are problems in the marriage, the need is sometimes there to talk to someone for help. There might be an urge to lean a little more on opposite-sex friends for comfort during these times. This could lead to unplanned emotional or even physical engagement. You can avoid this by leaning on your female friends (for women) or male friends (for men) instead.

- Address unmet needs and unresolved anger in your marriage with your spouse in an open, honest, and timely fashion. By addressing issues before they get out of hand, you have the opportunity to resolve them before temptation with friends could occur.

The most important thing to remember with friends of the opposite sex is to make sure your spouse is aware of those friendships, especially if they are regular conversations. This will help you avoid any confusion. It's better to communicate and have discussions about friends like these early in the marriage to make sure you're on the same page. Hiding things like this could create suspicion in your spouse's mind.

Honor and treasure your marriage by not engaging in secret relationships that could possibly cause problems. This includes telephone conversations, social media, text messages, or any other communication that your spouse is not aware of. Having secret friendships could possibly hinder the intimacy you have with your spouse. In the long run, neither your spouse nor your friend deserves to be hurt as a result of the confusion that can be caused by a secret friendship.

Family Values

Knowing your family values will help you make a lot of decisions in your marriage, whether you have children or not. Family involves your nuclear family, which is you, your husband or wife, and your children, if you have any. Family also includes your extended family, which is your parents, grandparents, sisters, brothers, aunts, uncles, nieces, nephews, and other relatives. Family does not necessarily have to include blood relatives. Family can consist of people who love and support you and being around them makes you feel like you're home.

A lot of disagreements in marriage can be avoided if you know upfront where each of you stand regarding family. This means you, your spouse, and your extended family should know where you stand in your family circle. Make sure your extended family knows that you love and respect your spouse. They should never feel comfortable challenging the peace of your relationship. When your extended family sees the love and respect you have for each other, they will love and respect your spouse, too.

Make sure you and your fiancé are on the same page when it comes to family. For example, if you like to have family members visit your home often and your spouse doesn't, it can create problems between the two of you. If you're used to sharing your resources or finances with your family before marriage and your spouse doesn't, it might create problems with your household budget. Determine how close you want to be with your family and your spouse's family in terms of sharing time, space, and financial resources. Check to see if your fiancé feels the same way.

Consider which family values you want to uphold in your marriage. Our family values usually come from what we observed in the household we grew up in. If we experienced a tight-knit family, we would like to continue that in our own household. If we experienced negative situations like violence or absent parents, we want to try to avoid that in our own home. If we grew up in a two-income household, we're used to seeing Mom and Dad taking on financial responsibility. If we lived in a house where Dad worked and Mom didn't, that's an example we're used to.

Think about the values you would like to see represented in your family. Your values could include social, political, religious, work, moral, and recreational values. Here are some examples of values you might consider:

- Treating each other with respect and being courteous

- Both husband and wife working consistently for financial success

- Volunteering in the community

- Taking a family vacation every year

- Having a family pet

- Going to church every Sunday

- Making education a priority

- Having family game night

Knowing what you believe in as parents will help you raise your children, should you have any. Your children will have a stronger sense of what is right and wrong because of the values you instill in them. It will help them to feel connected to a family and less likely to be manipulated by outside influences or peer pressure.

Make a list of the values that are important to you. Be prepared to communicate these to your spouse to figure out how to integrate them into your marriage. As you spend time together, you will have more shared experiences as a family and allow you to get to know each other better. This will help you figure out what matters most to you as a family. Keep your values in mind as you make life choices together. As you live out your family values at home, it will influence the way you treat others outside your home.

If you are a blended family, you will need to consider how you will merge the facets of your individual family values. Ask yourself the following questions:

- *How does your parenting style compare to your spouse's?*
- *What type of discipline will you use for the children to instill your values?*
- *What type of motivation will you employ to promote self-esteem?*

Try your best to allow the parent-child relationship to happen naturally in your blended family. In other words, don't force the children to automatically treat you like you are their biological mom or dad. Give them time to get to know you. It will take time for them to know they can trust you as a parent. Instead of using aggressive authority with them, approach them as the loving parent you plan to be. Keep in mind that there's possibly no one as important to your new wife as her children. Nothing is as important to your new husband as his children. Your spouse holds their children in their heart. So, it's very important that you handle their children, who are now your children also, with love and care.

In a blended family, it's both the mother and father's responsibility to create a safe place for children to grow. Children's minds and hearts are fragile and influential. It's a great charge to be able to raise children in your home. Treat the charge you have with honor and respect. Do all you can to make the children feel loved and belonged. Don't hurt them. Don't manipulate them. Cherish them and give them as much pure love as possible so that they will know how to love purely when they go out into the world.

Your goal should be to get to know your new children in hope to grow closer together as a family. If they happen to grow to love you in return, that would be great; however, be patient with them as you get to know each other. There may even be times when your new children's behavior toward you is not kind. There are many possible reasons why this might happen.

- They might have a fear that you are trying to take their mom or dad's place in their life.

- Their mom or dad might be speaking negatively about you to the children in an attempt to prevent you from getting closer.

- They might be shy and hesitant to get closer to people.

When it comes to discipline, unity is the key. The children must know that both parents are on the same page. Even if you don't agree about the "why" of the discipline, you must come to a middle ground regarding the "how" to discipline. Display a unified front. That means that you should not argue in front of the kids when it comes to decisions regarding them. If they see that you are not on the same page regarding their discipline, they will tend to seek out the parent whom they feel will sway their way. Let the children know that you are both on the same page regarding their safety, even when you do not agree on certain issues.

When I first got married, I would secretly send money to my daughter. She was grown and living out of town and occasionally needed a little help financially. That is something I was used to doing when I was single. I didn't know how my husband would feel about it, so I did it secretly. He also did things financially in secret when we first got married. He had a secret banking account which used to be called a "mad money" account many years ago. After sitting down and talking through our financial plans, we realized that we were actually on the same page regarding helping our children and managing money. So, there was no need for either one of us to keep financial secrets anymore. We decided what our guidelines and boundaries would be for helping our children and other family members and it has worked out very well.

Blended families can be complex because everybody manages their household differently. There will inevitably be different parenting styles and values. What has always worked for my husband and I is for him to manage the relationship with his children's mom and for me to manage the relationship with my daughter's dad. All interaction with our exes is done between us and in our presence when possible. It's in everybody's best interest, especially the children, to make sure all interactions are as peaceful as possible. The best way to do that is to keep interactions with exes to a minimum and only concerning the children. Communication with exes should be limited as much as possible to prevent any confusion of roles in the new marriage. You are no longer married to your ex; therefore, you should now communicate in a different capacity. All communication should be solely regarding the children you two parent together. The children's best interest should always be at heart. Never sacrifice their mental or physical safety when you are communicating with exes.

Family values are the glue that hold a family together. Values influence the decisions people make. Take some serious thought about your family values. When you get married, a whole new family will be created with you and your spouse. His family will become part of your extended family. Decide which values you want your new family to hold when you get married.

Financial Values

Knowing your financial values is crucial as you move from single to married life. Not everyone will have the same values you do when it comes to managing money. With money being one of the biggest causes of marital discourse, this is one area you should scrutinize regarding your future spouse. **Money cannot buy happiness but lack of it to the point where you are struggling from day to day could impact your peace of mind.** The reason you should know your financial values is so you'll know whether they match your future spouse's. Defining your financial values means you know the level of money management you want in your life. There are three levels of money management—struggling, just getting by, and thriving.

Struggling

Struggling is when the amount of your expenses exceed the amount of your bills. It means that whatever your source of income is does not cover the total amount of your bills. So, each time you get paid, after you pay your bills, there is no money left for anything else. Sometimes you might not even have enough money to pay your bills so you have to ask someone for help or you get a cash loan. A cash loan is probably the worst thing anyone can do financially because they have a 100 percent interest rate. It would be better to call your debtors and negotiate your next payment. Most companies are willing to work with you on making payments if you will communicate with them. I don't believe anyone intentionally wants to struggle financially. Most of the time they find themselves in that position for unexpected reasons—job loss, lack of good paying jobs, high cost of living, only one income to depend on.

Just Getting By

Just getting by is when you are living paycheck to paycheck. The amount of your expenses is the same as your income. Your income covers the total amount of your bills, but you don't have any money left to do anything extra, like go see a movie, or shopping, or travel. With constant market inflation and lack of high paying jobs, this is not an uncommon level of money management. Sometimes people have to get two or more jobs for extra income.

Thriving

Thriving is when your income covers all your expenses *and* you have enough money left to do other things, like traveling, shopping, helping others, and saving for the future. This is the ideal situation, but it usually takes years to get to this status, unless you're fortunate enough to thrive early in life. It usually takes higher education or training and planning to get to the thriving status. With hope, planning, and determination, this is an attainable goal for anyone who desires to thrive.

I've seen couples in all of these situations. None of these should determine whether or not you are happy in your marriage; however, it does help with goals and daily household management when you're on the same page of money management. If one person is barely getting by because of their impulsive and multiple credit card purchases, it could have a negative effect on the person's budget and goals who is thriving financially. It can become a source of arguments when your money management values are completely different.

Here are some tips for attaining financial success as a couple.

- First and foremost, you have to be on the same page regarding finances. Set your financial priorities together by making a list of the financial goals you want to accomplish. Some examples are buying a house or saving for retirement. It's important that you are on the same page regarding finances because this will be the foundation for all your financial decisions. When there is discord in your financial priorities, there will be limitations in your financial success as a couple.

Openly discuss your individual financial goals and then create a combined list that you both are comfortable with.

- Create a monthly budget and stick to it. Having a budget allows you to identify how you spend your money *before* you spend it and will help you stay within your spending limits. Be sure to include activities like travel, eating out, and gifts in your budget. Having these items in your budget will prevent you from feeling constrained in your spending. Review your budget together regularly to make sure you're still on the same page with the allocations. Make adjustments when needed to account for any new income or expenses.

- Manage your debt as a couple, even if it existed before you married. Your credit rating can be negatively impacted by your spouse's debt even if it existed before you married. The amount of money you pay monthly in interest charges will also be impacted by your spouse's credit because the interest rate is based on your credit rating. When my husband and I got married, our credit was not bad, but it was not excellent. Through the years we both increased our credit scores by working together to pay off the debt we incurred individually before we married. We paid more than the minimum amount due on our credit cards and eventually became credit card debt free. We now pay cash for all our major purchases. We would not have been able to accomplish this as quickly as we did if we did not work together and "adopt" each other's debt.

- Monitor your credit reports closely. Due to recent legislature, you can now receive your free credit report annually. Keep a close watch on each of your credit reports to make sure there is no fraud activity. Monitor your credit score and take action to increase it by paying your credit cards on time; paying off credit card debt as quickly as you can; and disputing any items on your report that shouldn't be there. When you pay off your credit card balances, leave the cards open. Closing the credit cards could reduce your credit score. The higher your credit score is, the better your chance of gaining a low interest rate on major purchases like mortgages and vehicles. A high credit score will often prevent you from having to make a down payment on major purchases also.

- Save at least 10 percent of your income monthly, if possible. If your budget does not allow for 10 percent, save as much as you can and increase the amount as your pay increases. Having a savings account will serve as an emergency fund and prevent unexpected cuts in your budget spending.

- Invest in your company's retirement program if they have one. Some companies will match your investment amount. For example, for every five percent of your paycheck that you deposit, your company will invest an additional five percent. If you're not employed by a company, seek the help of a financial planner for advice on financial institutions that offer investment accounts. Start by investing as much as your budget can afford and increase the amount as your pay increases. The earlier the two of you start saving money for your retirement years, the easier it will be to have a retirement lifestyle that you both hope for when it's time.

- Realize that you may have tough times. Even though you might have a budget, a savings account, insurance, and debt management strategy, you might still have some tough times. Unexpected losses like unemployment or reduced work hours could occur. During these times is when you draw on each other for strength to be able to manage the situation. Stay close to each other as you discuss innovative ways to push through the unforeseen loss, get back on your feet, and keep things moving.

Know Your Triggers

Knowing your emotional triggers is a big part of knowing yourself. An emotional trigger is an action, sight, sound, smell, or touch that causes your mind to flashback to a particular event in the past and causes an intense internal reaction. The emotional trigger stirs an uncomfortable feeling within you and may even provoke you to anger or sadness. Usually when someone experiences something that triggers a negative memory, he/she will emotionally react to the recollection. The reaction could be visible by others around at the time or it can be internal and hidden within.

One example of a trigger is hearing a song that reminds you of something that happened in the past. For instance, when I hear a particular song, it reminds me of a pet I had as a child. When I was eleven years old, I had a cute little puppy that was white and fluffy named Snowflake. Somehow Snowflake got away from the house while we were outside playing. Later that evening while we were settling in for the night, a friend rang our doorbell and told us that Snowflake had been hit and killed by a driver. The song "Gypsies, Tramps, and Thieves" was playing on the radio at the moment we got the news. From that time on, every time I heard that song, my heart would ache, and I would feel the same sadness I felt the day Snowflake died.

There are other triggers that remind me of pleasant things. Every time I smell Tabu perfume, I think of my grandmom because that was her favorite fragrance to wear. There's even a perfume that triggers memories of an elementary school teacher I had. I don't know the name, but when someone passes by with that scent, I think about her.

Sounds, scents, a touch can all be emotional triggers. A sound trigger could be a song, a loud voice, glass breaking, sirens, racing cars, a train, or specific words that stir an uncomfortable feeling within you. A scent trigger could be cigarette smoke, alcohol, a certain perfume, or a certain food. A touch trigger could be a certain physical touch, someone tapping you on the shoulder from behind, or the way someone walks past you.

Emotional triggers can wreak havoc in a marriage if they are not managed properly. Those triggers that cause very strong emotions within you can cause you to react in an unexpected manner. Knowing your triggers and how to manage them when you recognize them will help you manage your emotions. As you learn to identify the triggers that spark negative emotions, you'll be able to address them as they come.

A trigger that causes very strong emotions within me is a loud voice. When someone speaks to me in a loud and hostile voice, it provokes the emotion of anger within me. Knowing this, I immediately brace myself when someone talks loudly and aggressively to me. I pace my breathing and turn my thoughts to compassion and empathy instead of assuming the other person has a bad motive. I listen carefully to try and understand the message underneath the yelling, and then I attempt to respond in a tone of voice that I hope they will mimic.

I've learned that being proactive in planning how you will respond to your triggers will help you manage those situations. To be proactive in knowing that yelling is a trigger for me, I visualize how a discussion might go when I know I'm about to enter a difficult conversation. I prepare words that will hopefully prevent the conversation from escalating and getting worse. The more I use this technique, the better I get at managing the emotional trigger. I have learned that a soft answer really does turn away anger in difficult situations. The main focus I have during times when my emotions have been triggered is to avoid saying something I will regret later.

Be aware of your emotional triggers. It will take time, but you will eventually learn how to manage them when you feel certain emotions being provoked. Those emotions and feelings of uncomfortableness will clue you to immediately start working internally to manage your reactions. With time, as you gain more experience in situations that trigger your emotions, you will get better at managing them.

Know How to be Kind to Yourself

Knowing yourself means knowing how to be kind to yourself. Being kind to yourself involves loving and accepting yourself, forgiving yourself, and maintaining self-care.

Loving and Accepting Yourself

Being kind to yourself means loving yourself in spite of your flaws. We should constantly work on ourselves to try and get rid of our flaws while at the same time knowing we'll never be perfect. There is nobody in this whole world who is perfect. We can try as hard as we can all day, every day to be perfect, but the truth is, God is the only one who is perfect. If we focus on our weaknesses or flaws, it could cause us to have insecurities. To constantly remind ourselves or be reminded of our flaws by someone else could make us feel down on ourselves. Self-criticism or criticism from someone else could hurt our self-confidence.

I used to be hard on myself because I felt I could never be as good as other people at various things. I felt I wasn't good enough or smart enough. This insecurity affected my motivation to attempt things I wanted to try. I was comparing myself to other people and creating false expectations in my mind. When I finally realized my insecurities were because of my own thoughts and beliefs about myself, I was able to build my self-confidence.

Once I stopped comparing myself to others and accepted my own strengths and qualities, I began to love and accept myself. I even accepted my flaws because my flaws are part of who I am. I thought of all of the characteristics that make me who I am—good qualities *and* flaws. I believe that God created me to fill a specific place in this world. I have to be myself in order to fulfill God's purpose for my life.

Loving and accepting yourself means you know and love your personality. There are so many different types of personalities in the world. There are personality assessments that have been created to help people discover their true personality. Generally speaking, most personality assessment results show four different personality types—outgoing and talkative, reserved and quiet, analytical and logical, warm and sensitive. Assessment results show that you have one of these personality types or a cross between two of them.

Knowing your personality type will help you understand yourself better and will help you to love who you are. It will help you understand why you react to certain things in a certain way. Personality assessments are fun, and some assessments can even show you what personality types would be a good match for a strong personal or working relationship.

Loving and accepting yourself means you acknowledge your weaknesses and continue to work on them, but you do not beat yourself down. You should not allow anyone else to beat you down either. Don't be hard on yourself. Love and accept your personality. Work on diminishing your weaknesses. Love and accept yourself so that you'll be able to love and accept your spouse and others.

Forgiving Yourself

Being kind to yourself means forgiving yourself for the mistakes you made and even things you did intentionally. Sometimes we make bad choices in life. We find ourselves in situations where we give in to indiscretion. We know to do the right thing, but we end up doing the wrong thing sometimes. I believe everybody makes mistakes at some time or another, but we should learn from our experiences and eventually make better choices. There are certainly things in my past that make me cringe when I think of them. I am so thankful that I survived the bad choices I have made.

Part of being kind to yourself is to forgive yourself for the choices you made that you are not proud of. You might ask yourself if you would make the same decision if you could do it all over again. Whether you would or not, the fact is that it is already done. What's done is done. It is in the past now. If someone else was involved, and they were hurt by your action, hopefully you sincerely apologized to them. If you didn't apologize, consider whether now is a good time to do that or if it's best left alone.

I felt guilt for years for something I did to a friend of mine. It was something that happened many years ago in the 80s but I still felt bad about it. I saw her recently at a funeral and apologized to her for what I had done. The shock on her face told me she had no idea of what I had done. At that moment, I realized I shouldn't have mentioned it to her and not only that, I should have released it from my mind a long time ago.

Not forgiving yourself for past mistakes, bad choices, or just intentional indiscretions can cause unnecessary feelings of guilt and regret in your life. If you have things in your past that you are not proud of, pray and ask God to forgive you. God is loving and merciful and He will forgive you if you ask Him to. The moment you admit your fault to God and ask forgiveness, you receive it that very moment. There's no need to carry the guilt after that.

Let go of all guilt and shame. Feelings of regret can weigh you down and paralyze you from living life to the fullest. When thoughts and memories of past carelessness enter your mind, dismiss them. Remind yourself that you are forgiven. Maybe you were in a different state of mind then. Hopefully, you will not do it again, knowing the trepidation you feel about it now. God has forgiven you and no longer remembers. Forget all about it and go on with your life. The fact that you survived the indiscretion means that you have another chance to do things right in the future. Don't look back, keep moving, and try to make better decisions going forward.

Maintaining Self-Care

Being kind to yourself means making sure you do things to take care of yourself. Taking care of yourself means engaging in activities that help you maintain your mental, physical, and spiritual health.

Mental health is the condition of your psychological and emotional well-being. It includes how we think, feel, and behave. Physical health is the state of being free from illness or injury. Physical health includes your diet, weight, dental health, personal hygiene, and sleep. Spiritual health is that part of us that is composed of our personal values and beliefs and provides purpose for our lives. It is the core of who we are.

I cannot emphasize enough the importance of self-care, before and after marriage. Having "me" time plays a big part in self-care. "Me" time is time you spend doing things you enjoy doing as opposed to doing something *with* or *for* others. "Me" time is time to recharge or reset. "Me" time can interchangeably be called self-care. Self-care is essential to inner happiness.

Self-care involves eating well, sleeping sufficiently, meditating, or doing whatever relaxation techniques work for you. When you are in a relationship it doesn't mean you have to give up the things you love doing, as long as they do not cause you to neglect your marriage commitment. Hopefully, the things you love doing will be some of the same things your spouse enjoys doing. But you also need to make sure you make time for the things you love doing that contribute to your self-care, even if those are things you do alone.

Make self-care a priority in your life because it contributes to your happiness. Self-care is just as important as your relationship. Make a list of hobbies you enjoy doing. Plan some time at least once a month when you indulge in these hobbies. Schedule solo dates with yourself only. Cultivate a spiritual practice where you spend time praying or reading God's Word. Get an exercise routine that's right for you and fits into your schedule. These are all ideas for self-care.

Doing things on your own will help you stay connected to yourself and cultivate a sense of who you are. It will also keep your relationship fresh because you are renewed when you take care of yourself. Participate in activities that help you to grow and expand in new directions. Growing and learning new things will help you nurture the relationship with yourself and with your spouse. Self-care activities help you to rejuvenate and gives you a fresh new outlook on life.

Some things you can do to rejuvenate are:

- Go for a long walk in a safe area.

- Take an art class or other class you're interested in.

- Visit the library.

- Get a massage.

- Go fishing.

- Get a manicure / pedicure.

- Sit on your porch and just relax.

- Meditate.

- Take a yoga class.

- Listen to your favorite music.

- Sit in a private area and read a book.

Now is a good time to let your fiancé know you will occasionally need "me" time. By letting him/her know early in the relationship, it won't come as a surprise when you mention it later. Some people might not understand why you need "me" time. If your fiancé has a hard time with it, assure him/her it's actually something you need to be able to come back to the relationship stronger and better. "Me" time is rejuvenating and is one of those things that keep the marriage alive. Be careful not to abuse "me" time from your spouse. As with everything in marriage, it should always be done with respect.

Here are some boundaries to set for your "me" time to make sure you uphold the boundaries of respect and love in your relationship:

- Always let your spouse know when you will have your "me" time. This ensures your time alone won't interfere with plans he/she may have had for you together.

- Always let your spouse know where you are in your "me" time. For safety purposes, your spouse needs to know where you are and an approximate time to expect you to return home. By doing this, he/she will know where you are in case any emergency situations occur.

- If your spouse is uncomfortable with you having "me" time, discuss the reason why. If it is because of trust issues stemming from a previous relationship, assure your partner of your faithfulness. Take shorter periods of "me" time until he/she is more comfortable. As time passes, confidence and security will build. If your spouse's insecurity is because of something you have done, let your partner know he/she can call you at any time while you're out. Make sure you answer the calls. Rebuilding trust takes time, but it will eventually happen.

- "Me" time should not involve anyone or anything that would cause you to dishonor your marital commitment or reputation.

Being kind to yourself means setting boundaries for your life to make sure you are healthy. It means taking care of yourself to make sure you are physically and emotionally fit. It means rewarding yourself when you have personal victories, becoming your own cheerleader and motivator when you accomplish something, whether it's big or small. Being kind to yourself means protecting your time from people or activities that drain you of your strength and motivation. It means not judging yourself when you make mistakes. When you make a mistake, assess the situation to figure out where you went wrong but do not condemn yourself and beat yourself down.

Being kind to yourself means doing those things that are most important to you. One thing that is very critical to successfully transition from single to married life, is to continue to do those things that reflect who you are. That means you have your own individual interests, hobbies, apart from the ones you have with your spouse. This will help in so many ways during your marriage.

Having your own hobbies will help maintain your interest in one another. Having someone in your life that you are with day in and day out keeps things interesting when you also have interests of your own. It gives you something new to share with each other from time to time. It helps each of you to grow as you learn and then share that knowledge with each other.

Believing the Best about Yourself

Being kind to yourself means believing the best about yourself. It's hard to believe the best about yourself if you are constantly criticized by someone, including yourself. It's important to know how to identify the difference between constructive feedback and criticism. Constructive feedback is feedback that someone gives you to help you improve. It's called constructive because it builds you up and makes you better and stronger. Criticism is a negative comment made with the intention to reveal a flaw or make a person feel bad about him or herself. Constant criticism can affect a person's self-esteem. After hearing repeated negative comments about yourself, you could eventually start believing those comments.

I know a woman who was a happy, vibrant, and friendly woman for years. She married a man who constantly berated the way she dressed and acted. Every time I saw them, I noticed how he constantly put her down. It seemed like there was nothing she could do right in his eyes. I watched her personality slowly change through the years from an energetic happy person to a reserved and quiet one. I believe constant criticism did this to her.

Take a moment to think about your future spouse. Does he/she criticize the things you do, or encourage you to do better? If your partner is constantly telling you what you are doing wrong and never encouraging you to do better, that's not a good sign of someone you should spend a lot of time with. Sometimes people use criticism and then say afterwards that they were joking. Well, it might be a joke to them, but those words are going through the air and into your ears and heart. You'll eventually start believing those things about yourself because you hear it repeatedly. Then you'll start feeling bad about yourself and that low self-esteem will affect how you interact with people, how you perform on your job, and how you do everything else.

Take careful consideration about the person you are going to marry. Are their words discouraging or encouraging to you most of the time? Be kind to yourself and only accept the best for your life.

The more you know about yourself, the better prepared you will be for marriage. When you are fully aware of who you are and what your vision is for your life, you will be able to share your true self with your spouse.

It is important for you to know yourself so that:

- You will stay true to who you are, even after marriage.

- You'll know how to encourage yourself when times get rough.

- You'll have a moral compass to guide you when making tough decisions.

- You'll know how to communicate who you are to your future spouse.

Actions to Take to Know Yourself

1. Pray and ask God what purpose or void in this world you were created to fill. There's a space in this world that only you can fill, and people that only you can reach. Ask God what that space is and then look for His answer daily in all your interactions.

2. Take some time alone, look in the mirror, and ask yourself who you are. Be honest with yourself about your strengths, weaknesses, likes, dislikes, and what really makes you happy.

3. Grab a sheet of paper and write the following:

   a. List two words that describe the type of person you are.

   b. List your top two strengths.

   c. List two things in life that make you happy.

   d. List your top two life values.

   e. List two things you will not compromise under any condition.

4. Write a personal statement of who you are, using the information from step three. For example, my personal statement is:

   I am a unique and joyful person who is great at planning and organizing activities. Funny TV shows, gospel music, and sunny weather make me happy. The things I value most in life are my prayer time with God and balancing my time and energy for mental and physical rest. I will not compromise my life values for anyone.

5. Keep your personal statement in a safe place and revisit it often as a reminder to stay true to who you really are. It's important to maintain your individual personality as part of your husband or wife role.

6. Make a list of things you like to do that make you happy. Pick a day of the week or month when you schedule time to do these things.

Scriptures to Read to Know Yourself

For as he thinketh in his heart, so is he. (Proverbs 23:7a)

So, God created mankind in his own image, in the image of God he created them; male and female he created them. (Genesis 1:27)

Now you are the body of Christ, and each one of you is a part of it. (1 Corinthians 12:27)

I am the vine; you are the branches. Whoever abides in me and I in him, he it is that bears much fruit, for apart from me you can do nothing. (John 15:5)

But to all who did receive him, who believed in his name, he gave the right to become children of God, (John 1:12)

Prayer to Pray to Know Yourself

Father God, thank You for creating me. I know You created me for a reason, to fill some void in this world that only I can fill. I pray that You lead me and direct me in the path that You have for me. Show me the work that You have for me to do and give me the strength and wisdom to do it. Let me never be ashamed of who I am but to be confident in the person You created me to be.

Thank You, God, Amen.

Chapter Two

♡

Get to Know Your Future Spouse

Now that you know a little bit more about yourself, it's time to learn as much as possible about your future spouse.

As you get to know your fiancé, evaluate your two personalities and lifestyles and ask yourself, *How does this person fit into my life? Am I taking on new challenges that will help me or hurt me?*

No one will ever really completely know their spouse; however, you should know basic information before you get married or else you won't really know who you are marrying. I've seen so many couples who found out shocking information about their spouse after marriage because they simply did not ask important questions *before* marriage.

As you get to know your future spouse, take a mental note of the discoveries you make. Take time to think about who he/she really is. Ask yourself if his/her personality traits, habits, lifestyle, behavior, and attitude are things you can live with. Find out if his/her goals and dreams coincide with yours.

If there is something about your fiancé that is unacceptable to you, please don't think you are going to change him/her. **Marriage should be a merging of two different personalities who are willing to accept each other's personality.** You shouldn't try to make the other person act a certain way. The couples I observe who are thoroughly enjoying life are those who don't try to impose restrictions on the other's personality. They completely respect each other's style and encourage each other to be themselves.

There are couples who seem to be completely opposite personalities and you wonder how they got together and even how they make it. I believe couples with opposite personalities thrive because they complement each other. They're like batteries—it takes the negative and a positive part of the battery working together for full blown power. With couples, one person's strength makes up for the other person's weakness. With this type of collaboration, you will always win as a couple.

My husband and I have completely different personalities. Our approach to certain situations is different. We have different views on some issues. Our communication styles are not the same. It's ironic that our personalities are different though because we have a lot in common and enjoy doing the same things. We've learned that the things he's strong in are weak areas for me, and the areas I'm strong in are weak areas for him. Even in household chores, there are things he doesn't mind doing that I don't like doing and things I don't mind doing that he doesn't like to do. We're a great team because of our differences. I don't try to impose my personality on him, and he doesn't try to impose his personality on me. We don't always agree on how the other does certain things, but we accept each other's style and fully support each other.

As you get to know your future spouse, be open to his/her strengths and weakness. Accept them for all their characteristics. Don't downplay any of your partner's strengths and weaknesses because they will all play a part in your relationship.

I've talked to couples who have major conflict with things like money decisions or disciplining their children. They are constantly fighting over these issues. When I asked them if it's something they discussed before marriage, they said they didn't talk about it. I strongly encourage every couple to get premarital counseling before marrying. Premarital counseling usually covers those major areas that come up in marriage.

Before you get married, figure out what things are important to your lifestyle. Once you identify those things, discuss them with your fiancé to make sure you're on the same page in those areas. One of the things my husband mentioned to me before we got married was that his family is very important to him. He said he stays in touch with his family pretty regularly and they are a priority in his life. Since I love spending time with my family also, we were on the same page with family values. There is no problem or conflict when we decide to travel to visit family because we both realize how important family is to both of us.

There are other things that took time for us to manage. Timeliness was a big area that we had to adjust to. Whenever we scheduled a trip to visit family or other vacations, we set a time to leave home. If the scheduled time to leave was 2:00, my husband would have the luggage in the car the night before and would be waiting at the garage door at 1:45. His philosophy is that if you are on time for any event, then you are late. I, on the other hand, would still be walking around gathering last minutes items that I wanted to put in the bags that he already loaded in the vehicle, saying goodbye to the dogs, and basically taking my time. I didn't see 2:00 as a "hard stop." This was frustrating to my husband, and I couldn't understand why. In my opinion, he was treating our vacation trips like an urgent military mission. When he explained his theory about timeliness, I understood and actually like the idea of getting to events early. So, going forward, I would set my time to be ready to leave at least one hour earlier than our scheduled time. This gave me time to move around and do last minute things. I eventually got used to leaving early.

Know Your Future Spouse's Personality

Part of getting to know your future spouse is getting to know their personality. What makes them tick? What makes them happy? What frustrates them? It's important to get to know your partner because if there is something you're not on the same page with, you'll need to ask yourself if it's a deal breaker or not *before* you get married. Whatever you do, don't go into the marriage thinking that you will change their mind about a certain thing. Make the decision regarding your marriage based on how your relationship is today. In my experience and observation, the good things and the concerns about your fiancé only magnify when you get married. The reason for that is simply because you are much closer and more personal when you move in together.

With some things, the best way to get to know your spouse is to observe them from a distance. You should ask questions to get to know them; however, observing them is a way to form your own opinion.

Here are some ways to get to know your spouse through observation:

- Watch how they interact with their family, especially their parents and children, if they have any. Are they kind, loving, gentle, and giving, or harsh, cold, callous, or hostile?

- Watch how they treat the server at restaurants when you eat out. Are they respectful, kind, and friendly, or demeaning, condescending, or rude?

- Watch how they interact with your family. Are they warm, open, and friendly, or withdrawn and try to isolate you from your family?

- Watch how they interact with people less fortunate than them. Are they compassionate and sensitive to their condition, or act superior and judgmental?

- Listen to how they talk about people at work. Are they sociable and diverse in their acceptance of people, or do they make discriminatory remarks about certain groups of people?

Quietly observing your spouse-to-be in all of these situations can possibly give you clues about their attitude towards other people. In general, you should see signs that the person you are going to marry has the same convictions about showing kindness to others and that they are comfortable with you showing kindness to others.

There is a great sense of freedom when you are able to completely be yourself in a relationship. One of the things that caused me to fall in love with my husband is that he completely accepts me for who I am. Not only did he accept me, but he also encourages me to be myself and to pursue my dreams.

When someone is in a relationship where they don't feel free to be authentic, they'll feel tied down, in bondage, or in chains. Give your spouse-to-be the freedom to be who they are. Accept them for who they are—the good parts and the bad parts. Yes, you will discover bad parts about your spouse, just as he will discover bad things about you. We all have weaknesses, bad habits, and faults. If we can't be ourselves at home, where can we let our true self show?

Unconditional love is when you love someone even when they have sides that are unlovable. You can have unconditional love when you focus on the positive things about your spouse. Don't dwell on the negative things. And, whatever you do, don't mention the negative things. No one likes to hear criticism. Everybody knows their short-comings and does not need to be reminded of them. As you seek to understand your future spouse, look for their good features and qualities, and above all, love and accept them for who they are.

Know Your Future Spouse's Goals and Dreams
Knowing your future spouse includes knowing his/her goals and dreams to see if you fit into that picture. They might not even know their goals and dream yet. Even though they might not know what their vision is yet, they do have something inside—they just don't know how to verbalize it. As you get to know your spouse,

pay attention to him and his interests. Pay attention to the things she mentions.

These are some clues as to what their hopes and dreams are:

- *How does she interact with other people?*
- *What type of activities is he involved in? What are his interests?*
- *What does she spend most of her time doing?*
- *What does he get excited about when he's participating in or talking about it?*

Ask yourself how you see yourself fitting into their picture. What skills or attributes do you have that would help him pursue his purpose in life? A wonderful thing about marriage is that you have someone to share your hopes and dreams with. And it's a bonus if they are able to help you in some way. Above all, be supportive of your spouse's goals and dreams. You should be their biggest supporter. No one should cheer your spouse on louder than you do. Encourage them to reach for their dreams.

More than likely you won't have the same exact dreams as your spouse. Since you are two individual people, you will more than likely have different goals. This is fine. If you do have the same goals and dreams, that would be great. But if you don't, hopefully your goals won't conflict with each other. This could cause serious issues if your goals cause you to move in opposite directions. If your goals are completely different, make sure you work to prevent them from clashing. Some couples are in conflict about whether to have a family and if so, how large. If the partners are of different religions, they may struggle as to how their children should be raised.

Some singles have moved around a great deal and like the freedom of mobility. What if they marry someone who deeply believes in being close to their original family and can't imagine living away from their support circle? Or, what if one person wants to travel abroad every year while the other person would rather stay at home? Talk about your individual dreams and goals to see how they can be woven together while at the same time allowing for each person to grow.

Know Your Future Spouse's Strengths and Weaknesses

Knowing your future spouse's strengths and weaknesses is a big part of getting to know him/her. Knowing your spouse's strengths means bringing out the best in him/her at every opportunity possible. Help your spouse present their best self to the world. Give them books to read on subjects they're interested in to help reach their goals or dreams. Give them articles related to their interests. Give them words of encouragement.

Knowing your spouse's weaknesses is more about what you do not do rather than what you do. Don't bring up their weaknesses to them—they already know them. Don't judge them or condemn them for their mistakes. Give them space to do better or get better.

One of the most important things you can give your spouse is the freedom to be who he/she is. This even includes weaknesses. No one likes to be controlled or scrutinized. As you go into your marriage, be aware of those areas that your spouse might be insecure about. When you observe those weaknesses emerging, don't voice your disappointment in a condescending way. If it's necessary to say anything at all, tell them in a loving way. Otherwise, let them work out their own struggles. Remember that we all have weaknesses. With that in mind, we don't have room to criticize someone else for their faults. We can, however, lovingly help them as they find their way through their weaknesses.

Part of knowing your spouse's weaknesses is knowing his/her triggers. A trigger is an action or lack of action that provokes a negative response in someone. Those feelings or negative responses are usually feelings of fear, anger, or sadness. The feelings are usually a result of something horrible that happened in the person's past.

Usually something they have not healed of yet. Examples of a trigger for your spouse could be:

- Yelling at them or the children, if you have any.

- Talking to your spouse like they are a child.

- Mentioning your spouse's mom or dad.

- Bringing up private information about your spouse around other people.

- Criticizing your spouse's looks or abilities.

- Correcting your spouse in public or around friends and family.

You may not understand why your spouse has the triggers he/she has, but you are responsible for being careful about creating those triggers. If you know your spouse has a fragile relationship with his/her parents or a sibling or someone else, be sensitive to his/her feelings by not mentioning anyone that could trigger those negative emotions.

Knowing your spouse's strengths and weaknesses is about focusing on their strengths and encouraging them to be their best; and also, being aware of their weaknesses without drilling them into their ears every chance you get. It's about giving them the freedom to express themselves and fulfill their purpose in this world with your support.

Know Your Future Spouse's Religious Preference

Knowing your spouse's religious preference is a big part of getting to know him/her. Religious differences can make or break a marriage. Take a look at your future spouse's religion and yours and determine if they are a good match. Are you affiliated with a religious order, and is your future spouse affiliated with a different religious order? If so, look at the doctrine, rituals, and convictions of both religions to see if there are any conflicts in worship days, diet restraints, seasonal holidays, rules, and customs.

If religion is important to you and spending time in a local church or in religious activities is a priority for you, find out if your fiancé has the same priorities. If he/she does not have the same priorities, find out if it will cause any conflicts in your time together if you participate in those activities.

As I mentioned earlier, faith in God is a very important part of my life and my husband's. It's our experience that having that faith foundation and regular prayer time is the foundation and saving grace for our marriage.

If you choose not to go this route, consider what you will have as the foundation and "glue" to keep your marriage together during the tough times. There might be times in your marriage when you will need a mediator to help solve some issues that come up. Ask yourself:

- *What level of devotion do we desire to have with God?*
- *If not God, what do we have in our life that is greater than ourselves that will keep us strong?*
- *What will keep us on track as a couple when times are hard?*

Your future spouse may identify more with the word "spiritual" instead of "religious." Spiritual is more about faith in God not necessarily affiliated with any organized religion. Your fiancé may be in pursuit of spiritual growth for his/her life rather than committing to attending religious activities.

If you find out that your future spouse neither has an interest in religion or spirituality, ask yourself if you want to spend the rest of your life with someone you are not unified with spiritually or religiously so. I do know couples who have completely different religions, or one participates in religious or church activities and the other doesn't. For the most part it seems to work for those couples who are not on the same page in this area.

I do have a dear friend who met a guy who was everything she ever dreamed... at first. They dated for over a year and were engaged to be married. The more she learned about him, she found out he was involved in a religion whose teachings were completely opposite of her beliefs. The religion he was heavily involved in promoted discrimination against certain races of people. Her church taught that God is love and loves everyone. My friend did not agree with her fiancé's form of religion and beliefs and did not want any part of it in her life. She called off the engagement and left the relationship.

As you get to know your future spouse, find out if they are part of a religion, church, or spirituality whose teachings are beliefs you can live with. Find out if their religious or spiritual beliefs will divide the two of you or help to create a bond.

Know Your Future Spouse's Values

Getting to know your future spouse involves knowing their values. The values you share will make a huge impact on your day to day living.

Moral Values

I knew a lady who married a guy who constantly lied to people. He would lie to his friends about his cars, how much he made, and even cheated on his taxes by claiming dependents he didn't have. Not only that, he would purchase stolen items like big screen televisions, video game consoles, and jewelry. It wasn't long before she figured out he would also lie to her about things. Habitual lying is a personality disorder she didn't find out he had until after they got married. It's one of those things that's kind of hard to identify in the dating phase.

Honesty is a moral value that is important in marriage. **Honesty builds trust.** A lack of honesty can erode the marital relationship pretty quickly. Other moral values like integrity and loyalty are equally as important. Before you marry, make sure you have a good sense of your spouse-to-be's moral values or lack thereof. Everyone has weaknesses and bad habits that we are all working to get rid of. Make sure your fiancé's habits do not involve activity that could land you or him/her in jail or the hospital, or worse yet, threaten your life. Look a little deeper into his/her life and find out:

- *Do we have the same moral values and if not, is this something I can safely live with?*
- *Will their lack of values in this area interfere with the solidarity of our marriage?*
- *Does this difference in moral value prevent me from trusting him or her?*
- *Is this lack of moral value a danger to my health?*
- *Does it interfere with our marriage?*
- *Could it possibly be a danger to our children's well-being?*

Moral values may not seem like a big deal to some and it might not be a deal breaker, but it's certainly something to consider when you think about how it could affect your future. If your future spouse has no moral values regarding illegal activity, then you could end up alone for years while they are in prison. Find out how your fiancé feels about any areas of concern you have regarding their values. Ask them what they think about unethical and illegal activity such as theft, fraud, selling controlled substances, assault. It's better to risk offending them with the question now instead of being surprised after marriage.

Family Values

Family values are values to be traditionally learned or reinforced within a family, such as moral standards and discipline. The family circle is such an impactful element of most marriages. At one time or another, you will interact with your extended family. It's important to set expectations early in the marriage regarding family values. Knowing your future spouse's family values will help to set the expectations.

Figure out where they stand when it comes to family.

- *Do they want to visit with family frequently or just every now and then?*
- *Do they want your family to be involved in your life—gatherings, dinner, birthday parties, holidays—or would they rather keep those just within your nuclear family?*
- *Do they want to be able to help family members when they need it—loan money, give them a place to stay—or do they want to set a rule that you never do either of these?*
- *Are they open with discussing personal matters with extended family, or would they rather keep family business inside the home?*

I know so many couples whose lives are in turmoil because of extended family. This is usually because the husband and wife are not on the same page when it comes to extended family. One person likes to spend a lot of time with family, but the other doesn't. One person gives money to the family when they need it, the other one thinks they shouldn't. One person tells all of their personal business to the family, the other is private. There are different issues that can cause problems in extended families. The main source of this problem is that expectations regarding family values were not set at the start of the marriage.

Make sure you know exactly where your fiancé stands with family values before you get married. Find out if you're on the same page. Set some guidelines and expectations for extended family *before* you get married.

Relationship Values

It's very important to know your fiancé's relationship values before you get married. When I say relationships here, I'm referring to associates, connections, and friends. The way relationships are managed can have a huge impact on your marriage. If there are areas that are important to you regarding relationships that are not important at all to your spouse, it could cause major conflicts in your marriage.

Knowing your future spouse's relationship values involves knowing which relationships, specifically friendships, they want to continue into your married life together. The relationships they continue will in one way or another become part of your married life. For that reason, it is critical that you and your partner are on the same page when it comes to which relationships and friendships you both will have.

It's an understatement that good friends are hard to find. It's kind of rare to find friends you connect with on many levels, have a special bond with, and can confide in. Friendships should be cherished and held on to for as long as possible.

On the other hand, friends can have either a negative, positive, or neutral effect on your marriage. One area I've seen married couples have problems with is the husband or wife who secretly continues to be friends with an ex. While this type of friendship might be fine when you are single, it could cause problems in your marriage. Find out if your spouse will continue to have friends of the opposite sex after you get married. Make sure you're on the same page about this so that there's no confusion later.

If you and your fiancé decide that it is okay to have friends of the opposite sex when you get married, it's important to have boundaries around those friendships. Boundaries will help prevent causing any confusion in your marriage. Some of those boundaries should be:

- Be open and honest with your spouse as to whether you are comfortable with them having friends of the opposite sex or not. Letting them know early in the marriage will show them how you feel and give them the opportunity to address any insecurities you have about the friendship.

- Let your partner know that you need open and honesty about his/her friends of the opposite sex. Conversations with his/her friend should not be hidden and should not only happen when you are not around.

- Show your trust for your spouse by not accusing him/her of any extramarital activities with his/her friends. If they are openly sharing their communication and interaction and not keeping any secrets from you, don't impose any feelings of doubt on them. Don't fuss unless you have factual reason to.

- If at any time you are uncomfortable with the friendship between your partner and his/her friend, address it with him/her immediately. Talk about your feelings in an open, honest, and timely fashion. By addressing your apprehension before it gets out of hand, you are giving your spouse the opportunity to resolve it before you react in a hostile way.

- If you feel that you need friends of the opposite sex to live a fulfilling life, and your spouse-to-be is strongly against it, be aware that this disagreement will cause conflict in your marriage.

The most important thing to remember with friends of the opposite sex is to make sure both of you are aware of each other's friends, especially if they are regular conversations. Hiding things like this could possibly create suspicion in each other's mind.

Financial Values

Financial management tends to be a sensitive area in a lot of marriages. The reasons I believe it creates issues is because people either don't discuss it before marriage, they're not completely honest when they do discuss finances, or they choose to ignore concerns.

A friend of mine met a wonderful man that she fell in love with. He was the perfect gentleman—opened doors for her and brought flowers when they went out on dates. They went for romantic walks in the park. They had good discussions about life and had a lot of things in common. She liked that he always dressed well and wore nice cologne. She loved spending time with him. He eventually proposed to her during one of their romantic walks. As months passed, my friend found out her fiancé shares a banking account with his daughter. His daughter is 36 years old, but he still supports her financially. When my friend asked him if he planned to continue supporting his daughter after marriage, he said yes. He said she is his only child and she has children and needs financial help. Since sharing a banking account with his daughter was a deal breaker for my friend, she broke off the engagement and the relationship. This was only one of the financial concerns she had about him. He also had questionable side jobs that sounded unethical to her.

It's important to find out the financial status of the person you are marrying. If you are currently struggling financially, you might not want to marry someone who is also struggling financially unless the two of you have a plan to improve your situation. Find out what their financial values are. It could be embarrassing for them if you ask them about this directly but assure them that you are asking for the best interest of both of you. Tell them that circumstances would not be ideal for your marriage if you are barely getting by. There are ways to discreetly get an idea of your future spouse's financial values. Consider the following:

- *Do they ever pay for the meal or other activity when you go out, or are you the one who pays most of the time?*
- *Do they pay with a credit or debit card? Multiple credit cards could indicate a lot of debt.*
- *Do they live in an apartment or a house? They might be saving money for a house if they're in an apartment.*

- *What type of things do they say about money? Do they always talk about being broke? Do they mention how they are saving money?*
- *Do they often say they don't have enough money to pay their bills?*

Because money management is such a huge factor in marriage, it's crucial that you know where your future spouse's financial values are. Take some time to get to know how they think about money, income, working, and even retirement.

Know Your Future Spouse's Triggers

Getting to know your future spouse's emotional triggers is part of getting to know him/her. An emotional trigger is an action, sight, sound, smell, or touch that causes a person's mind to flashback to a particular event in the past. The emotional trigger stirs an uncomfortable feeling within him/her and may even provoke them to anger or sadness. This trigger usually causes a negative reaction. You may or may not even notice the reaction.

It would be very helpful to find out what your future spouse's emotional triggers are. Some conflicts can be prevented if you're aware of each other's emotional triggers. As you learn to identify the triggers that spark negative emotions, you'll be able to address them as they come.

I have a friend who found out after years of marriage that her husband's trigger was any type of feedback or criticism. Any time she gave him feedback on something he did, like hanging pictures on the wall or dressing the baby, he would get angry. She didn't realize this was a trigger for him until he hung a picture on the wall for her one day. She asked him to move the picture again a few inches towards the center of the wall. In response to her request, he snapped and ranted about how she always criticizes him and doesn't appreciate anything he does. Later, after he cooled off, she talked to him about why he responded that way. She found out in their discussion that he was constantly criticized by his dad during his childhood. He was told repeatedly by his dad that he never did anything right. After my friend's discussion with her husband, she understood why he got so angry when she asked him to fix something he did. Criticism or feedback was a trigger for him.

We are all unique individuals with different life experiences. Be sensitive to your fiancé's emotions as you get to know them. Be patient in areas where they have emotional triggers that you don't understand. As you learn their triggers, be proactive in planning how you will respond to those triggers. For example, if a certain physical touch is a trigger for your spouse, be aware of that as you touch him/her.

If a certain tone of voice like loudness or specific words are triggers, think about what to say and how to say it before you speak. Set a goal in your mind to purposely have a mature conversation. Use words that encourage productive communication. Express how the issue at hand impacted what the two of you are trying to accomplish. Don't blame him/her for problems that come up. In heavy discussions or arguments, your goal should be to figure out *what* is right in the situation, not *who* is right.

Be aware of your emotional triggers and those of your future spouse. Try your best to remember to avoid the triggers and therefore avoid the problems that could occur. Avoiding triggers will help to create a safer environment for your partner as you build your lives together.

Know How to Be Kind to Your Future Spouse

Knowing how to be kind to your future spouse means loving and accepting him/her for who they are, forgiving them when they make mistakes, and encouraging them to maintain their spiritual, mental, and physical health.

Sometimes we can be more kind to perfect strangers than we are to our own spouse. What I mean by that is, we use politeness and good manners when we are in public, but we don't do the same at home. We say "excuse me" when we cross over someone to sit down but we don't say "excuse me" when we step over someone's leg at home. We say "please" and "thank you" to the salesclerk but we don't do the same at home. I've observed husbands and wives treat their friends and even strangers so much nicer than they treat their spouse. I believe they don't even realize they're doing that. I know one lady who screeches, smiles big, and opens her arms wide to hug her male friends when she sees them. I wonder if she does the same when she greets her husband at home.

Your spouse deserves the same nice treatment you give to others. Demonstrate common courtesies in your communication with your spouse. Say "please" when asking for favors like a glass of water. Say "thank you" when they do something nice for you, even with something simple like passing the salt during dinner. Try using the same gentle voice you use with strangers to communicate with your spouse. Offer to get your spouse something to eat or drink when you can.

Take the time to think of some ways you can show kindness to your spouse. Do this on a regular basis and it will eventually become a habit. Kindness shows respect for your spouse and also shows them that you care about them.

Here are some ways to show kindness to your spouse.

- Offer to give them a cold drink when they're working in the yard.

- Run a bubble bath for them after a long day of work.

- Massage their feet after a long day.

- Fix their plate along with a nice cold drink.

- Surprise them with a small gift, for no reason at all.

- Speak to them in a soft and pleasant voice.

Being kind to your future spouse also means focusing on their positive characteristics. Look for the best in your spouse on a regular basis. Be diligent about digging for the gold nuggets in their personality. This will help you live a happier, more peaceful life. Everybody has positive attributes. Take the time to look for the positive attributes in your spouse. Your confidence in your spouse might be what they need to motivate them to be their best. You can reinforce their strengths by looking for the good in them. How you see them will affect how you treat them. If you look at your wife as a loving, supportive wife, you will treat her that way. If you see your husband as a strong, protective husband, you will treat him that way.

Here are some ways to look for the best in your future spouse:

- Make a list of their positive attributes, no matter how big or small.

- Constantly remind yourself of their positive attributes.

- Consider their real intentions in those situations when they are being unlovable. Assume the best and not the worst.

- Think about your own weaknesses before you criticize them.

- Don't compare your spouse to your ex. Wipe away all past memories, concerns, and issues and approach your spouse with an open heart and mind.

There is a quote that is attributed to Abraham Lincoln that says, "If you look for the bad in mankind expecting to find it, you surely will." Grandma would say it like this, "Baby, if you go looking for something bad, you're gonna find it." Well, I used to wonder about this statement because I felt that if something was going on, I need to know about it. But I learned that it wreaks more havoc on *me* to go looking for something bad than it does *him*. It takes time and negative energy to spy, snoop, and look for something bad. It's like the analogy for digging dirt—you're going to get dirty.

To look for something in your future spouse means you have a lack of trust in them. That lack of trust may be warranted by a previous experience with him/her or someone else. Whatever the reason, it only does harm to yourself when you go looking for something. It's harmful to you because it takes an attitude of distrust to even pursue the "dirt" you are looking for. It's also harmful to you when you find something that incriminates them. So rather than spending the time and energy it takes to look for something bad, use that time to look for the best in him/her. Use that time to focus on your own interests and hobbies. The time you spend looking for something wrong could be spent doing more productive things with your life. Nothing good will come from looking for dirt. The more you dig, the dirtier you will get.

"Spying" on your future spouse is not healthy. It's detrimental to your peace of mind and could eventually affect your mental and physical health.

Here are some reasons you shouldn't check up on your spouse (after marriage):

- It takes precious time and energy to snoop into your spouse's activities. That time and energy could be spent doing something positive and productive.

- You are mentally antagonizing yourself with worry and fear. Worry and fear never solved any problems. It can lead to physical illness.

- You should pray and ask God to keep your spouse from infidelity and to take care of you. Then trust God to protect both of you.

- What's done in the dark will come out in the light eventually. If anything underhanded and disloyal happens, it will surface. Be prepared to handle the challenges that come in a mature way.

- Divorce is not an option (unless there's physical or mental danger). Ask yourself what you will do with the bad information if you find it? If you don't plan to divorce, don't go looking for reasons to divorce.

Filtering Your Words

The most powerful tools you have for being kind to your spouse are your words. The words you speak to yourself, to your spouse, and to others have so much power. Words can affect your attitude about yourself and your future spouse. When you speak, words can stir up emotions. If you speak down about yourself all the time, you'll eventually begin to feel emotions of sadness and inferiority. It's the same with your future spouse, if you constantly speak negatively about them, they will eventually feel bad about themselves. If you only mention your spouse's weak areas to others, they will look at your spouse in a negative way.

Speak words to your future spouse that spark motivation for them. To be able to do this, you have to speak encouraging words to yourself first. Remind yourself of good experiences you have had in your life. Don't focus on past failures. Try to have an unconditional love for yourself. Learn from your failures but move past them and focus on making a brighter future. Use words that build yourself up and also build up your spouse.

I know someone whose conversation always sound so negative. She always talk about bad news and bring negative feelings to those around her. She is pessimistic. She will find a way to shoot down other people's expectations and hopes. Every time you say something, her response is negative. Almost everything you say, she'll contradict it. If you say the sky is blue, she'll say, "No it's more like gray." If you say the sky is gray, she'll say it's blue. I'm pretty sure she doesn't realize she is doing this.

Think back over your conversations with family and friends and ask yourself if you usually speak positive or negative about things. If you suspect that you might be, ask a few close friends for their opinion. Speaking negative words will not help in creating a pleasant relationship with your future spouse.

Be careful what you say and how you say it. In my experience, the things I speak positively about tend to get better and the things I complain about seem to get worse. I believe it's because when I hear myself speak something, I either believe it more and then I act on it, or it sounds ridiculous and I dismiss it. This has been true in every area of my life and especially in marriage. When I speak positively about a situation instead of complaining or fussing about it, it always turns out better. When I dismiss the negative thoughts and focus on the positive, and then speak about it in a positive light, it always turns out better.

Speaking positive words does not mean you ignore issues that need to be addressed. It means you think and speak positive about the situation until it is resolved. Rather than jump to conclusions or assume the worst, think through your words before you speak them. Visualize what you are going to say to your spouse that explains how the situation made you feel. Don't use accusatory or blaming words.

When difficult situations come up, remind your spouse of the commitment they made regarding the circumstances. Consider the fact that they might have even forgotten about the commitment or might not have known the action would offend you. Always look for their true intention, rather than in what you see. Ask questions to try and get to the source of the problem. Then use words that express how you feel without condemning them.

Before you speak, think about what you are going to say and how to say it. Don't make matters worse by reacting in a hostile or violent way, or by using horrible words. Sometimes you have to bite your tongue until you can think of a nicer way to say something.

Once your words are heard by others, you can't take them back. Ask yourself: are you saying what you are about to say to help them or hurt them? If you really want to help them, you will say it in a way that they will receive it.

People remember what you say for a long time. Relationships have been destroyed by things someone said that they wish they could take back. If you say something often enough, they will eventually start believing it. This goes for positive and negative things. The more you talk about things the stronger it gets—good and bad.

Respecting Each Other's "Me" Time

Being kind to your spouse means respecting their "me" time. "Me" time is critical for individuals because it helps foster healthy relationships. A healthy relationship happens when two individuals are emotionally healthy. "Me" time increases emotional health because you're participating in activities that make you happy.

"Me" time is when you spend time alone, doing things you enjoy doing as opposed to doing something with or for others. "Me" time is time to recharge or reset. "Me" time could also be called self-care. Self-care is essential to inner happiness. Give your future spouse time and space for self-care when they need it. Don't feel slighted when they tell you they need some "me" time. Just know that they are doing what they need to do for self-care. Have some hobbies of your own so that you're not sitting around moping for your spouse. You'll have more interesting conversations when the two of you have hobbies of your own.

Make sure you let each other know when you want your "me" time. It might even be helpful to have scheduled "me" time, for example, going to the nail salon every third Saturday or going fishing every fourth Saturday. My husband and I have a lot in common and we do almost everything together. We also have our own hobbies that we enjoy doing alone. My husband knows I love to read, so I spend "me" time reading. I know he loves to fish which is something I do with him occasionally, but he fishes in his "me" time.

Your future spouse may not express the need for "me" time. Not everybody needs it and may even feel it is inappropriate when you're married or in a relationship. If your spouse-to-be says they don't need "me" time, then don't feel that you have to give them that. At the same time, don't feel slighted if they *do* express a need for "me" time. By all means, it's not a personal vendetta against you if your spouse needs "me" time every now and then. Try to be understanding and sensitive to your future spouse's need to do some things on their own every now and then.

Boundaries for "Me" Time

As you respect your spouse's "me" time, be sure to uphold the boundaries of respect and love in your relationship.

- Let each other know early in the relationship that you will occasionally need "me" time so that it doesn't come as a surprise when you mention it.

- Schedule the "me" time in advance and at an agreed time with your spouse so that it does not interfere with any plans you have together.

- "Me" time should not involve anyone or anything that would cause you to dishonor your marital commitment or reputation.

Being kind to your future spouse means giving him/her the space needed to stay in touch with who they are. Having "me" time helps them accomplish this. "Me" time helps them to maintain their self-care so that they are mentally, physically, and spiritually fit. When they are free to be their authentic self, they are able to fulfill their purpose in this world.

Know How to Manage the Unfortunate Surprises

Getting to know your future spouse will mean that you will need to manage the unfortunate surprises you find. Life is full of surprises and you will have a few within those first few years. There will be wonderful things you discover about your spouse that you never imagined. Some examples are things they're exceptionally good at doing like cooking, fixing things, talking to people, managing money, parenting, driving, among other things.

You will also have unfortunate surprises about your spouse after marriage. Unfortunate surprises are those disappointing things that you will learn about each other after you get married. Some of them might even seriously threaten your marriage. Rather than give up or call it quits on your marriage, consider reacting to the unfortunate surprise in a way that is productive and promising for your future.

I know a lot of marriages that experienced unfortunate surprises including my own. It can be very disappointing and also feel like betrayal. For some reason there are just some things we don't find out or realize until after we marry the person we love. This might be because the person didn't feel it was important to mention, or they purposely didn't mention it for fear that the other person wouldn't marry if they knew. Or, maybe the person saw signs and kind of suspected it but chose to ignore it. Whatever the case, it's quite common to learn disappointing and sometimes shocking and disturbing things about your spouse after you get married.

Some of those unfortunate surprises I've witnessed in married couples are:

- She is not as affectionate as he thought she would be.

- He has bad credit.

- She still communicates with her ex on a regular basis.

- He's addicted to pornography.

- She has a secret banking account.

- He has a child she didn't know about.

- She has an enormous amount of credit card debt.

- He has a hard time keeping a job or just don't like to work.

- She has a criminal record.

- He has problems managing anger.

- She lied about having a college degree.

- He's paying child support.

The unfortunate surprises you encounter in your marriage might not be as drastic as these, but you might experience some nonetheless. When unfortunate surprises surface, there are several reactions I recommend: evaluate the solidarity of your marriage; give your spouse the space they need; maintain your self-confidence; and be open and honest about your feelings.

Evaluate the Solidarity of your Marriage

Take an inventory of your marriage and ask yourself if what you have together is worth pressing forward with the surprise. Make a list of the positives in your marriage and weigh them against the negatives to determine which weighs the most. If there is more good in your marriage than bad, it is probably worth the effort it will take to work through the surprise. If, on the other hand, the bad outweighs the good, consider getting professional help with the situation. Some situations require the assistance of a licensed professional counselor to learn how to communicate and work through the issues.

Before you react to the unfortunate surprise and make any major decisions, do the following:

- Give yourself time to process the news in your mind and heart.

- Consider what the other person's real intention was in keeping this information from you. Was their intent to hurt you? More than likely not. Even though it may have resulted in hurting you, it was most likely not their intention.

- Put yourself in his/her shoes and ask yourself how you would want them to respond. Use the same mercy and empathy you would want for yourself.

- Plan a mature response to the situation. Don't let your reaction be worse than the news itself. Don't say or do something you will regret later. Express your anger, hurt, and disappointment about the news in a clear and discreet manner. Your goal is to let him or her know and understand why you are hurt and to prevent it from happening again. If you go overboard in your reaction, you will not be able to productively resolve the issue.

I know a situation where a husband found out his wife regularly had lunch with a male colleague at work. In rage, he went to her job and confronted the person she had lunch with. She ended up losing her job which put them in quite a financial bind. His action was overboard and caused undue stress on their marriage and financial status. This is a case where the reaction was worse than the infringement. If he had handled it by talking to her about it instead of going to her job, they could've come to an agreement and she would still be employed.

More than likely your spouse has been dealing with the guilt of holding the unfortunate surprise. Don't make matters worse in your reactions to the secret. Manage your emotions and prepare to have a logical discussion about how to move forward. Consider how it will affect your lives together in the long term. If you can see the two of you working through the issue, fully supporting each other, being patient, getting professional help if needed, then by all means give it all you have. If you choose to work through the issue, do it with your whole heart, with no turning back.

Give Your Spouse the Space Needed

If it's a personal struggle your spouse has such as pornography, lying, or alcohol, allow him/her the space needed to get treatment and work through it internally. You can't force anyone to change, but if you give them the space and emotional support needed, they can get better. It's important that you provide as much emotional support as you can when your spouse is trying to work through a personal struggle. Treat them the way you would want to be treated if you had a major weakness that they just found out about.

When the unfortunate surprises arise, don't freak out like it's the end of the world. I know a woman who found out her husband was calling another woman behind her back. There was no sexual affair or even meeting in person. He just called the other woman on a regular basis. When the wife found out, she freaked out and got angry and kicked her husband out of the house. He rented another apartment for months while trying to work things out with his wife. He assured the wife that the other woman was just a friend but kept it secret because he knew how she felt about him having female friends. They agreed to do counseling and eventually reunited. The separation caused a huge dent in their financial planning. It could have been avoided if the husband was open and honest with his wife and if the wife didn't react so extreme in kicking him out.

Consider giving your spouse the space they need to work through their personal struggles. If they repeatedly fall back to the same blunders, require them to get the professional help they need to be able to move forward productively in your marriage. If their habit is abusive or harmful to you and/or your children, seek safety away from them until they recover.

Maintain your Self-Confidence

One strategy that will help you deal with the unfortunate surprises is to be confident and secure in who you are as an individual *before* marriage and *after* marriage. You're probably wondering how being confident in who you are helps with surprises like these. Well, when you have interests or hobbies that occupy your mind and energy, you are not overtaken with grief and abandonment when the unfortunate surprises pop up. In other words, you won't feel that all is lost when you receive traumatic revelations about your spouse. Because you have activities you enjoy that help you maintain who you are and your self-confidence, you are not completely dependent on your spouse for emotional well-being. When your whole being is not dependent on your spouse, you are able to stand in your own strength during difficult times in your marriage.

Marriage requires 100 percent effort. You should constantly seek to be giving to each other and to look out for each other's best interest. You should put your marriage first before any and all relationships, because biblically speaking, you are two people who have become one. You should make sacrifices and compromises to make your marriage work and to keep unity in your marriage. You should be committed to one another in the good times and bad. To be able to commit to the marriage, you have to be a healthy person yourself and be able to stand in your own strength during the tough times. You can accomplish that by knowing and loving yourself and by having individual interests or hobbies of your own. There might be times in your marriage when things seem hopeless. During these times, draw from the inner strength of who you are and occupy yourself with those activities that bring you hope, while you attempt to work things out with your spouse. Maintain your self-confidence and walk like a victor, not a victim of the unfortunate surprises that may arise.

Be Open and Honest About Your Feelings

Some things you just choose to forget. Perhaps your spouse's secret was a thing of the past and he/she did not want to mention it to you. However, if they have fallen back into a habit, or if it is something that will affect your future as a couple, it should not be kept secret from you. Be open and honest about your feelings regarding the unfortunate surprise. Don't sweep it under the rug and ignore it. Deal with it now either by talking through it together or with a counselor. Failure to express how you feel about it now could possibly cause you to explode later in one way or another.

Openness and honesty about the things both of you struggle with or things that could possibly resurface is crucial to building trust in your marriage. As you communicate and work through unfortunate surprises, your relationship will become stronger.

I know a guy who was convicted of a felony over ten years before he met his fiancé. Years ago, he got into a fight with one of his co-workers because his co-worker threatened his life. He fought the guy to protect himself and others involved. The co-worker filed charges against the guy. Because they were on government property, he spent some time in prison which caused him to have a felony record. He hesitantly told his fiancé about the record but was surprised at her response. She responded with great appreciation for his openness and honesty and did not let the record influence her decision to marry him.

If there is something in each of your pasts that could impact your future together, it's only fair that you let each other know. Something like a criminal record could affect your ability to get a good job. Not having a good job could impact your family income and thus your family's well-being.

I know a woman who told her fiancé she had a degree in a field of work that typically has an excellent job market. After they got married, she went years without being able to find a job. Her husband found out she didn't actually have a degree at all. She had to resort to taking low paying jobs. Now, they are constantly struggling financially, which causes strain on their marriage.

Let your future spouse know that they don't have to be afraid to share their secrets with you. It's better that you know now before marriage than to find out later after marriage. Ask them to give you the opportunity to decide if their secret is something you want to live with or not.

You're the only one who knows within yourself what you are willing and able to handle in your marriage and what you cannot handle emotionally. When you have discussions about the sensitive areas or private struggles, be honest with yourself and your spouse as to whether that is something you want to live with for the rest of your life. Don't trick yourself or your spouse into thinking that things will change, because they may not. Make the honest decision as to whether you want to diligently hold on to your marriage and manage the unfortunate surprises in hope that things will get better, or to give up and start life over as a single or with someone else who will also have unfortunate surprises. If you hold on, things will more than likely get better in the end.

It is important for you to know your future spouse so that...
- You will have a good idea of who you are marrying.

- You'll know how to encourage and support them.

- You'll be aware of their emotional triggers.

- You'll know how you add balance to each other's lives.

Actions to Take to Get to Know Your Future Spouse

1. Pray and ask God to show your future spouse's true personality to you. Then, open your eyes, ears, and heart to what you see in him/her. Listen and watch without any expectation except to know the real person.

2. Take a few steps back from the relationship and assess who your future spouse really is. Suppress your emotions and physical attraction in order to take the time to get to know him/her. Emotions and physical attraction can cloud your perception of your fiancé. It's easy to see them through rose-colored glasses when you are initially enamored with someone. Be honest with yourself about your strengths, weaknesses, likes, dislikes, and what really makes you happy.

3. Grab a sheet of paper and write the following:

   • List two words that describe the type of person you think your fiancé is.

   • List your fiancé's top two strengths.

   • List two things (not people) in life that make your fiancé happy.

   • List your fiancé's top two life values.

   • List two things your fiancé will not compromise under any condition.

4. Write a personal statement using the information from step three. For example, my personal statement is:

   "My fiancé is a person who is great at communicating and working with his hands. Being around family and listening to gospel or old school music make my fiancé happy. The things my

fiancé value most in life are his children's wellbeing and making a good life financially. My fiancé will not compromise his good name or credit for anything."

5. Keep your fiancé's statement in a safe place. Revisit the statement as you get to know him/her to get an idea of who he/she really is. As you get more acquainted, ask yourself if his/her personality (strengths and weaknesses) is something you could live with the rest of your life.

6. Do not seek to change your fiancé or anticipate them changing after marriage. You must be willing to accept them the way they are now—good and bad.

Scriptures to Read to Get to Know Your Future Spouse

Be devoted to one another in love. Honor one another above yourselves. (Romans 12:10)

Be kind to each other, tenderhearted, forgiving one another, just as God through Christ has forgiven you. (Ephesians 4:32)

Let the morning bring me word of your unfailing love, for I have put my trust in you. Show me the way I should go, for to you I entrust my life. (Psalm 143:8)

Prayer to Pray to Get to Know Your Future Spouse

Father God, I ask for Your permission to marry this man (or woman). I also ask that You show me their true personality. Let me not be led by my own physical desires, but help me to have my eyes and ears open to what You need to show me. I am looking forward to the great things You have in store for us. God, I pray that You prepare our hearts for one another, that we will know how to love each other. As we get to know each other, give us patience and understanding. Help us to put You first and then put each other's needs and desires before our own as we learn each other. Father, please strengthen us and deliver us from our shortcomings. Help us to grow as we encourage each other to use our strengths. Amen.

Chapter Three

♡

Shift Your Mindset for Married Life

As you continue to learn more about yourself and your future spouse, start thinking about how you will approach married life.

Right after you get married, there's a time period when you are gradually settling down into married life. Everything is exciting and new, and you are loving the fact that you are now living with and sharing your life with your husband or wife. Although the enjoyment of your new life is there, there are some areas where you will need to shift your mindset from single life to married life.

It might take some time to start thinking like a married person rather than a single person. Thinking like a married person means you now consider someone else when making decisions. When we are single, we get used to doing things on our own that we're still in autopilot when we get married. It takes a mind shift to move out of the single mindset to a married mindset.

The mind is a powerful engine. It controls every part of our being. Our thoughts can take us to higher heights and can also take us to deeper depths. **We can talk ourselves into something and we can also talk ourselves out of something in our mind.** We can control our feelings with our thoughts. How we react in different situations has a lot to do with our thought patterns. If you think positive thoughts about a person or situation, it will be easier to choose positive reactions to them.

There were mind shifts that my husband and I both had to make when we got married. There were certain things he was used to doing as a single man that he had to change his perspective on. He had to learn all over again that some things are perfectly fine to do when you are single, but they don't transfer into marriage very well. With me, the biggest shift was sharing my space. I love and cherish my "alone time" and it was a challenge to allow him into that space.

Through time and multiple mistakes, we learned that we have to consider the other person, even in private situations. It doesn't mean you don't ever have privacy. It means that you always consider how your actions would make your partner feel if they were there with you, or if they knew about it. It means respecting your spouse even when they`re not around. For every action you take, there are two people to consider—not just one. Before you make that move, stop and consider how your actions will affect the person you love.

Make sure you know what each other's expectations are regarding daily activities. There are many examples of mind shifts that may need to take place after marriage. Here are some I have heard:

- Getting used to someone else's things around the house.

- Going home at a decent time and not staying out all night.

- Tolerating bathroom habits like leaving the cap off of the toothpaste or leaving the toilet seat up or sleeping habits like snoring.

- Sharing a bathroom or closet.

- Having non-stop visits from friends who raid the refrigerator.

- Driving to events together when one person is always late.

These are all areas that might require a major mind shift and why it's so important to get to know your spouse as much as possible *before* marriage.

People outside of your marriage will try to impose behaviors and actions on your relationship that you have no interest in. Don't let anyone pressure you into treating your spouse a certain way. How you and your spouse interact with each other is your business only. Nobody else should be able to tell you how to treat your spouse. What matters is that the two of you are in agreement about how you treat each other, and that treatment should always be with love and kindness.

Shift from the Past

One critical mind shift for moving into marriage is to let go of all memories of past relationships. Whether the relationships were good or bad experiences, you shouldn't keep reliving them in your head. It will be very difficult to focus on the present if you're constantly looking at the past. One danger in not erasing memories of past relationships is that you could unknowingly treat your spouse as if they are your former partner. I've witnessed this in so many relationships.

- The wife who wanted her husband to do certain things that a former boyfriend did.

- The husband who took everything personal because his former wife belittled him.

- The husband who was unhappy with his current wife because she didn't do things his former girlfriend did.

- The wife who is treating her husband a certain way because her former spouse liked it.

- The husband who cheats on his wife because all his former girlfriends cheated on him.

- The wife who spies on her husband because all her exes cheated on her.

It's not fair to your current spouse to treat him/her as if they are your ex. We are all different in one way or another. We have to approach marriage with an open mind and open heart without comparisons. Don't look for similarities in your current and former relationships, whether good or bad. Start with a clean slate and get to know his/her unique personality.

A profound statement a counselor once made to me was "Don't give your husband apples because your ex liked apples. Your husband might like pears, not apples." I didn't realize I was doing that until she said that. This statement means that what works in one relationship may not work at all in another relationship. That also goes for things that *don't* work. What did not work in a previous relationship might work just fine in a new one. It all boils down to getting to know your spouse and treating them according to their preferences.

Shift to a Life Partnership

Shifting to a mindset of life partnership is advantageous in marriage. A partnership happens when two parties make a commitment to have each other's back, to stick together like glue, to have a unified front in the face of adversity, to not let anyone come between them.

One of the biggest things you can do to create unity in your marriage is to have each other's backs, no matter what the circumstance. A unified front creates a defense against possible external interferences to your marriage. It covers up any weak spots that could be exposed to potential attacks. The world does not need to see your marital issues. Any problems you have should be worked out in private or with a licensed counselor. Make the commitment internally and with your spouse to back each other up in life.

When one of you pursue goals of any magnitude, big or small, provide verbal support. Encourage your spouse to be their best in life. Speak good about them to your family and friends. Encourage them to do well at everything they try to do. Be their best cheerleader. If someone talks bad about them, tell them about their positive attributes. Don't allow others' opinion of your spouse tarnish your feelings for him/her. Stand on what you know is true about him/her. Know that everyone makes mistakes at one time or another. If he treats you well and is not abusive, and he's learning and growing, stick by his side with love, patience, and kindness. If she's faithful to you and is doing the best she can to be a good wife, stay with her, compliment her, and encourage her.

Be there for each other and assure each other that you are always there to talk through any issue. Try your best to make your spouse feel comfortable enough to talk to you about anything. There might be some embarrassing things your spouse will not want to talk to you about; but that reason should never be because you will judge them or laugh at them or kick them out of the house. Help your spouse to know that you are always there for them.

Shift from "My Resources" to "Our Resources"

Sharing resources is an important mind shift as you move into marriage. As you establish a life together, resources like time, money, energy, love, religion, friends, family, hobbies, and self-care will need to be prioritized. The amount of energy we place behind each one of these can be anywhere on a scale of very low to very intense. After marriage, it becomes like a circus balancing act to manage all your resources, especially when you have children.

When we are single, we can allocate resources according to our own needs and schedules. For example, if a resource is time, some people like to plan how they will spend their time in advance. Singles can set their schedule exactly the way they want to. If planning is something they have done for a long time, they might get frustrated with a spouse who likes to be spontaneous or likes to wait until the last minute to make plans.

What if going jogging every morning was something one person liked to do while they were single but now the person they're married to likes to lay in bed and cuddle every morning? Or, what about a couple in which one person loves to have lots of parties and social activities, but the other person would rather spend more alone time together. I've seen couples who fight constantly over this issue. When there is a huge difference in how much time to spend with friends, it could make both people in the marriage feel uncomfortable.

As the marriage matures, the couple will learn what is important to each other and will understand when to make the other person's desires a priority. This is when compromising comes in—taking turns in giving in to each other's desire in order to support the other person's enjoyment.

Shift from "My Money" to "Our Money"

Managing finances plays a huge part in the marriage mind shift. Money can be a source of stress in a marriage. This happens because there's a difference in spending beliefs and habits. Being on the same page in regard to finances can help keep a marriage strong and help you achieve some major goals. The best thing to do is sit down before the wedding and discuss both financial circumstances such as current income and debt, child support, college loans, and any concerns you have. Having an open and honest discussion about finances can get you started on the right foot.

What works for one couple may not work for every other couple. Things to consider are:

- *Will there be two incomes or one?* To help with this decision, ask yourself *what is our desired lifestyle, and do we need two incomes to accomplish that lifestyle?*
- *How will we monitor our income to make sure we stay on budget?*
- *Should we have joint accounts to make monitoring easier or should we have separate accounts?*
- *What should our spending habits be to help us reach our goals?*
- *What types of spending habits should we avoid so that we don't miss our targets?*

Deciding how you will merge your finances should be a top priority. Merging finances should occur *after* marriage, not before. Legally speaking, it's best to wait until after marriage to make major purchases like a house, car, or furniture. The reason for that is because you have legal ramifications that rule your financial assets when you're married that you don't have when you are not. For example, in a lot of states, when you buy a house, car, or other property when you're married, it is considered "community property" which means both of you own it equally. Whether the property is in your name alone or your spouse's, it is still considered community property. When you buy property and other assets together and you're *not* married, there are *no* laws that protect your right to the assets.

Another reason to wait until after marriage to merge finances is because you'll be listed as each other's life insurance beneficiary. When you are not married, your boyfriend or girlfriend is not required to list you as a beneficiary. If they were to die before you and the two of you have financial assets together, there's no guarantee you would receive the assets the two of you worked so hard for. You also might not have the life insurance benefit you would need to pay off any bills you accumulate together when you're not married.

It's exciting to be engaged to be married and it's tempting to move in together before the wedding date and to start buying things together. After all, you know you love each other and you're definitely going to be together because there's nobody else for you. It's smart financial management though if you carefully plan how to merge your finances first. Sit down and talk through the steps you will take to merge your finances *after* marriage. Don't be in a rush to get a banking account together until *after* marriage. Having a joint banking account requires complete trust in someone's commitment on all levels. It would be disastrous if you got joint banking accounts before marriage, bought a new car, or other major purchase only for your fiancé to suddenly disappear. Unfortunately, I've seen that happen to people I know. It may or may not have been a scam all along. We'll never know. But, what we do know is the victim's bank account is now bare and their credit is ruined… all because they didn't wait until *after* marriage to merge finance. Marriage legally protects you financially. Seriously dating or living together in most states does not.

Options for Merging Finances

Once you are married, there are three options for merging your finances—joint banking accounts, separate banking accounts, joint and separate banking accounts.

Joint Banking Account

A joint banking account is when a married couple combines their paychecks or other recurring income into a single banking account in both their names. Having joint banking accounts and managing your money together is an option that works well for many couples. Some couples may feel that sharing all aspects of their life, including the financial, is a significant gesture and a demonstration of transparency and trust.

My husband and I have used joint banking accounts since the very beginning of our marriage. We have found this method to be very productive in helping us to save money and reach financial goals. We maintain a budget of our total monthly income and expenses. We regularly do financial planning and vacation planning based on the balance of our joint accounts. We don't take a specific allowance. We both spend what we want based on our individual needs and wants, but we make decisions together on our major purchases.

In our house, we don't say "my money" or "your money." We say, "our money." This eliminates any feelings of inferiority as it relates to which one of us makes more money than the other. It also helps us see our joint account as one pot of money that we use for all of our money management and financial planning.

There are advantages and disadvantages of having a joint account.

Advantages of Joint Account

On a practical note, having a joint account can make managing the household's money easier since everything goes into, and comes out of, a shared account. There's no balancing act of trying to manage multiple accounts. Having a joint banking account simplifies your household money management.

Another advantage of a joint account is that you have two sets of eyes watching the bank statements. It's important to check your banking account regularly to make sure income and expenses are processed correctly. I can't tell you how many times we found incorrect and even fraud transactions in our account. With a joint account, there is a greater chance of spotting mistakes or identifying savings opportunities more often.

Having a joint account streamlines your legal affairs. In the event one spouse passes away, the other spouse will retain access to the funds in a joint account. This might not be the case when you have separate accounts. You might have to refer to a will or go to court to claim the money in individual accounts unless you are listed as beneficiary on each account.

Having a joint account is rewarding in more ways than financially. Not only does it help you to successfully build a strong financial structure in your marriage, it contributes to creating unity in your relationship.

Disadvantages of Joint Account

There are some drawbacks to having a joint account. One disadvantage is that it's hard to surprise each other with gifts. During those times we usually have to be creative in finding ways to hide those purchases. A joint account also limits your ability to have a level of financial independence you might want. If you desire complete freedom over your finances, a joint account will probably make you feel uncomfortable.

A joint account can be a disadvantage when spouses are not communicating with each other about their spending, especially when one spends a lot more than the other. This could cause an imbalance in the account.

Some couples don't like joint accounts because one spouse enters the marriage with more debt like student loans, credit cards, and child support that now must be paid with joint funds. It's best to be open and honest about all debt before marriage so you can decide together the best approach for merging your finances.

With a joint account, one of you needs to be designated as the "financial manager" of the house. The household financial manager's role is to regularly monitor the account(s) and make sure all the bills are paid on time from the joint account. The days of writing checks and balancing a checkbook are gone. Almost everything is done online. The household financial manager is responsible for checking the accounts regularly to make sure everything balances out.

Separate Banking Accounts

Some couples find that keeping their money completely separate works best for them. There are reasons why they make the decision to do this. Perhaps they're not ready for the huge commitment of having a joint account yet. Maybe they have other logical reasons for keeping their accounts separate. Whatever the case, there are advantages and disadvantages of having separate accounts.

Advantages of Separate Accounts

The biggest advantage of separate accounts is that you can buy whatever you want whenever you want. You can make crazy purchases if you want and nobody else can say a thing about it. With separate accounts you don't have anyone looking over your shoulder or questioning your purchases.

Another advantage of having separate accounts is that you can avoid some arguments and disagreements about finances. Some people regularly make impulsive purchases and don't manage their money very well. Sometimes they even spend money before they pay their bills and then realize later they don't have the money to pay all of the bills. Having separate accounts prevents banking discrepancies as well as arguments or disagreements that would take place because of this behavior.

If you marry someone who has a huge amount of debt such as credit cards, child support, or IRS payments, having a separate account allows you freedom from having to divide your finances to pay the debt.

Other reasons some couples have separate accounts is because one person makes much more money than the other and doesn't want to share. In some marriages, one person is a hard-core saver and the other person is a big spender. Some couples don't agree on financial decisions together, so they decide to manage separate accounts. In some marriages, there are simply trust issues when it comes to finances.

Disadvantages of Separate Accounts

The biggest disadvantage of separate accounts is that your funds are limited because there is only one source of income versus two. I know a couple who has separate banking accounts. They live in a beautiful house. Her income is much higher than his. She leases a brand-new luxury car every two years. He drives old trucks and has to buy one every two or three years because they break down on him. At one time he had to go weeks without a vehicle because he could not afford to buy another one. In this situation, I believe he would've been able to get another vehicle sooner if they had a joint account. Two incomes are better than one when you need to make major purchases.

It's hard to make informed financial decisions because you don't know what's in the other persons account. Decisions regarding major purchases, vacations, retirement, and helping other family members are difficult to make without knowing how much money you have to spend as a couple.

It's not a bad thing to have separate accounts if that's what works for you as a couple. As long as you agree on this method and there are no secret individual accounts, it should not be a problem. If you know this is the method you prefer, discuss it before marriage or at least early in the marriage so that your spouse is not surprised. It's not good to have any type of secrets in marriage and that includes banking accounts. Let your future spouse know about your preference to have an individual account. Let them know their name won't be on the account but they're welcome to see the bank statements at any time.

If you do decide to have separate accounts, make sure both of you maintain enough money to pay your share of the bills and contribute to savings. Split up mutual bills, such as the mortgage or rent, groceries, and utilities so you each have your own responsibilities. You may want to split the bills so that you both pay about the same amount each month, or the amount that's proportional to your income. Even though you have separate accounts, be sure to set financial goals together like a down payment for a home, college tuition for the kids, vacations, and retirement. Make sure you have a plan for handling emergencies and paying off debt you accumulate together.

Joint *and* Separate Banking Accounts

A third option for merging finances after marriage is to have a joint account for shared bills and savings and also have separate accounts for individual spending. The joint + separate account scenario is where there is one account where both spouses deposit their paycheck and they also have individual accounts where they deposit a certain amount each pay period. This is the most popular scenario I've seen couples use.

Advantages of Joint + Separate Accounts

An advantage of joint + separate accounts is that you can decide how much to contribute to the joint account. If one of you make considerably more than the other, you can contribute a percentage to the joint account to cover your share of the bills. This allows you the financial freedom you want while at the same time being responsible for bills.

Another advantage is that joint + separate accounts could make it easier to manage household bills and savings goals, while each spouse also gets to keep part of his/her financial life separate.

Many couples use this type of system. They create a joint account where their income is deposited. The joint account is where the bulk of their paycheck goes. They also have individual accounts where they deposit a certain amount each pay period. If you have your paycheck on direct deposit, you can set an automatic allotment amount for each of your accounts.

With this type of system, you are free to spend the money from your account as you wish without accountability from your spouse. You can buy surprise gifts for each other without the fear of them finding out. You can go golfing, out with friends, or anything else without having to monitor the bank balance for bills. The money in the individual account is yours to spend, no questions asked. Remember though that you must be willing to share your bank statement with your spouse at any time so that there are no secrets. Secrets can inhibit the financial trust you have with your spouse. Don't cause undue strain on your relationship by refusing to be transparent with your spouse about your spending habits.

Disadvantages of Joint + Separate Accounts

One disadvantage of having joint + separate accounts is that your funds could be limited in your joint account because you are only depositing a certain amount versus the full amount from each source of income. When you need to make major purchases and there's not enough money in the joint account, you'll have to decide how to pull from the individual accounts to make the purchase. This could create conflict if you can't agree on how much money to pull from each account. If this happens, revisit the financial goals you wrote together early in your marriage, and discuss whether the purchase aligns with your goals. When you're both on the same page about what you want to accomplish, it won't be hard to come to an agreement on how much each of you will contribute.

Another disadvantage might be that it may be difficult to make joint financial decisions because you don't know what's in the other persons account. Decisions regarding major purchases, vacations, retirement, and helping other family members are difficult to make without knowing how much money you have to spend as a couple.

Shift from "My Space" to "Our Space"

Determining how you use your physical space together is a mind shift that happens in marriage. Sharing space is a big step in marriage since statistics show that moving is one of life's top stressors. With some people, sharing space is no big deal at all, but with others, it's a huge step that is very challenging. When you are single, your space is your own—your closet is yours to use as you like, how you arrange the furniture in your rooms, and something as simple as how items are laid out on your tables can mean a lot to you.

When you are single, your house is set up the way you like it. There's a certain way you arrange things in your home that makes you comfortable. Then when you get married and move in together, things aren't always arranged the way you like them. This can be somewhat irritable and could take some time getting used to.

One example of sharing your space after marriage is the man who has been single for years and has his house decorated nicely with just the right amount of space in each room and on the walls. Then he gets married and they decide to live in his house. She moves in and hangs her floral paintings on the walls, places aquariums in every room in the house, turns the garage into a den preventing him from being able to park his car in there. This is a case where the home he once loved is now crowded with his new wife's belongings.

Another case is where a woman has lived alone for years. Now her new husband has moved in and he leaves cups and other dishes on the coffee table instead of putting them in the kitchen when he's finished. He also leaves his dirty clothes laying around the bedroom. This is something that goes against her standards of putting things up when you are finished with them. She doesn't like to see things laying around the house.

I know a woman who met a wonderful man. They had so much in common and had a great time whenever they went out on dates together. They both have a love for cooking and sports.

Things got serious with them pretty quick as they enjoyed spending time together. He eventually invited her into his home and that is when she found out he lived with two dogs in the house. Because she thinks it's disgusting for dogs to live inside, she decided he was someone she would never marry. She preferred not to have dogs in her living space.

If you are dating someone whose living space is completely different from what you are comfortable with, then seriously consider whether you would be happy living with them every day. **In marriage, your home should be a respectful merging of both party's space.** It should not be an invasion of each other's life. You should mutually decide how you will use the space you will be sharing. The key in managing the transition to a shared space is to communicate your concerns. Talk about your likes and dislikes concerning how you like to keep your home. As you talk, determine whether or not you're on the same page when it comes to housekeeping.

When my husband and I got married, we both had a complete set of household furniture, appliances, dishes, pots, pans, and home décor. We knew we only needed one set of most of the items so we decided which sets we would keep and which ones we would let go. Home décor and furniture were two areas where we had to negotiate what we would keep. There were items that he had that I did not want as part of our décor, but because they had sentimental value to him, we kept them. There were a few pieces of furniture I had for years that he didn't want to keep so we decided to replace them with new furniture.

Everybody has different decorating styles. Some people like to have every room in their house filled with furniture and every wall covered in décor. Then there are others who don't like a lot of furniture or wall décor in their house. They like open space. There are also people who love to keep their house immaculately clean. They constantly dust furniture, wash dishes, sweep and mop the floors to keep their house clean at all times.

I have observed extremes on both sides of the housekeeping spectrum. I have walked into homes where the woman of the house quickly instructed us to take off our shoes and adamantly advised us not to touch certain things or go into certain rooms. Her house was immaculately clean with nothing out of place. I was afraid to sit down when she offered us a seat and motioned to the sofa that she approved for sitting. I have also walked into the homes that I could tell had not been swept, mopped, or dusted in months. I had to step over items to walk around and move things to find a place to sit. The kitchen sink and countertops were full of dirty dishes. The trash cans were spilling over. I used to wonder why some people would keep their house so dirty, but one day I figured it out. One lady whose house tends to be unclean every time I visit told me that there are more important things in life to worry about than having a clean house. She said it's not one of those things that is at the top of her list to do or worry about. That's when it hit me—a clean house is just not priority to some people. In their mind, they have so many other things in life that are a lot more important to them. Cleaning house is not important to them.

When there are two people who have completely opposite housekeeping styles, there can be serious conflict. To be able to merge your space successfully, consider the following:

- Before you get married and move in together, take an inventory of all the items each of you have in your homes. Take note of your furniture, appliances, dishes, pots, pans, towels. Decide what you will keep and what you will give away.

- Before you get married and move in together, discuss how you want your home to look—an "Open" concept with a lot of space in between furniture and wall décor or a "Cozy" concept with heavily fitted furniture and wall décor. The concept you choose will be the foundation for how you decorate and will help you determine how many things to keep as you merge your households and decorate.

- If you can't agree on the design concept, choose a specific room for each of your preferred designs. In other words, if you like the Open concept, perhaps the kitchen or living room could have that design and the rest of the house could have your spouse's Cozy design. Above all, be respectful of each other's comfort. Home should be a place of comfort. It should be a place that you love coming to after a long day at work. It should be a place where you feel secure enough to lay down and sleep at night. Both of you should be comfortable at home. A rule of thumb is that if there is something about your home that makes one of you uncomfortable, you should consider not doing that. Maybe one of you feel that the house is cluttered. This can be very uncomfortable for some people. Clutter can cause anxiety and uneasiness in some people. If clutter is an issue, the two of you should discuss this and determine what things you can eliminate from the house to de-clutter.

- Find out what your future spouse's priority is with house cleaning. The best way to do this is by visiting their home and observing for yourself. If you ask them, you may or may not get a true answer. This is not because they are lying to you. It's because their view of a clean house might be different from your view. What they think is a clean house may be different from what you think is a clean house. So, in addition to asking them how they feel about keeping a clean house, make sure you make some surprise visits to their home to see how clean they keep it.

- Ask them how often they clean their house. This will give you an idea of how often they do thorough cleaning and how often they do the quick cleaning.

- If a clean house is top priority to you, let your future spouse know this. They need to know this is important to you so they'll know how to co-manage your house with you. On the flip side, if a clean house is not priority to you, let them know so they'll know what to expect when you get married.

- If a clean house is top priority to you and you know it's not for your spouse, be prepared to be the one in charge of making sure the house is clean. Just as the person who is strongest in managing finances is usually the financial manager of the household, the person who has cleaning as top priority should be the one in charge of making sure the house is clean. This doesn't mean that person is the only one who cleans. It means that person is the one who makes sure everyone knows when it's time to get things clean.

Actions to Take to Shift Your Mindset for Marriage

1. Pray and ask God to show you how to love your spouse just as you love yourself or more. Ask God to show you how to support each other's dreams and goals. Ask for wisdom in bringing out the best in each other.

2. Remember that marriage involves commitment to your newly merged relationship as one. This means you now think, act, and behave as "us" instead of "me." When you think in terms of "us," it makes it easier to show love towards each other's children from a previous marriage or relationship. It's easier because the children become "our" children in our mind and heart. When you think in terms of "us," it makes it easier to share your income with your spouse because it's no longer "my" money or "your" money but it's our money, even if you do have separate banking accounts.

3. Get to know your future spouse and make sure you are not marrying someone who will take you completely out of your comfort zone. It's one thing to have a completely opposite personality than the person you're marrying. It's another thing when your lifestyles conflict with each other. Your opposite personalities should complement each other. Your lifestyles should provide comfort, not conflict. If you have major differences in basic ways of living, you should consider whether you should put yourself in that situation or not. Don't set either one of you up for failure.

4. Once you know the basic lifestyle of your spouse-to-be, start training your mind to think like his or her wife or husband. Imagine how you will live as husband and wife. What do you envision for your marriage?

5. Commit your mind, heart, and body to your marriage. Prepare to honor your marriage in everything you say and do. Ask yourself, *What things or people do I need to eliminate from my life now to prepare for marriage?*

6. If trusting people is a challenge for you, start by putting your trust in God. Pray and ask God to help you to walk in love towards your future—in the good times and the bad. Ask God to keep your spouse from infidelity and to only have a desire for you. You might not ever get to a place of complete trust in your spouse. But do ask God to help you to be strong and confident in trusting Him. Then walk in faith and belief that He will take care of you regardless of what happens.

Scriptures to Read to Shift Your Mindset for Marriage

Brothers and sisters, I do not consider myself yet to have taken hold of it. But one thing I do: Forgetting what is behind and straining toward what is ahead. (Philippians 3:13)

Two are better than one, because they have a good return for their labor. (Ecclesiastes 4:9)

He who finds a wife finds what is good and receives favor from the Lord. (Proverbs 18:22)

So I say, walk by the Spirit, and you will not gratify the desires of the flesh. (Galatians 5:16)

Above all, love each other deeply, because love covers over a multitude of sins. (1 Peter 4:8)

Prayer to Pray to Shift Your Mindset for Marriage

Father God, I am getting ready to take a huge step in my life. I pray that You would prepare my mind for marriage. I pray that You will help me to surrender my life to the person I love and help me to be committed to our union. Instill a great sense of respect in my heart toward my spouse. Please remove all selfishness and insecurities. God, please remove all painful memories of my past. Renew my mind completely and help me to walk in newness as I spend the rest of my life with the person I am madly in love with. Fill my heart with love, hope, joy, and forgiveness as I start this new life with the one I love. Thank You, God. Amen.

Chapter Four

♡

Prepare for Lifelong Intimacy

After you have a good idea of who you and your spouse are, you'll be on your way to lifelong intimacy.

You will spend the rest of your life learning how to live in intimacy with your spouse. The reason I use the word "learning" is because you will experience lesson after lesson on how to love your spouse. When my husband and I got married, I thought I had it figured out this time. I told him, "Hey, I believe I know the key to a lasting marriage now. The key is to continue to date each other after we say, 'I do.'" I told him that if we continue to do the things we did before marriage to impress and delight each other, then we should have a great marriage.

Now that we have been married a while, we have found that continuing to date each other does make a huge difference in marriage, but intimacy still goes deeper than this. There's a level of intimacy that comes with time and experiencing different situations in marriage. The process of growing more and more into true intimacy is so exciting because you will grow to a new level with each lesson.

Understand True Intimacy

The truth about intimacy is that it means something different to each individual. When I think of intimacy I think of closeness, tenderness, affection, and warmth. The dictionary's synonyms for intimacy are belonging, closeness, inseparability, familiarity, nearness. I see all of these when I think of intimacy. Holding hands, kissing, or a long embrace by someone you love and who loves you could be considered intimacy. Intimacy is something that is enjoyable and gives pleasure to both parties involved. Intimacy is something that is welcoming and pleasant. If it's not welcoming and pleasant, it's not intimacy. Intimacy is something that happens within.

In my experience and observation of other couples, there is a level of true intimacy that is undeniable. There's a connection that is difficult to imitate, it just shines through. True intimacy shows in how you talk to each other and treat each other in daily interactions.

It's such a joy to know that you are now going to have a lifetime of intimacy with the person you are marrying. In marriage, you have someone to share your innermost thoughts, dreams, and fears with. This creates intimacy. You have someone you can trust with your secrets and concerns and who will hold them close to their heart and not share them with anyone else.

Showing your spouse that they can confide in you with their private matters and you will keep those things near and dear to your heart creates intimacy. Moments of hardship, triumphs, and challenges in life and in your relationship creates intimacy when you stick by each other's side. Opening your heart to your spouse and being vulnerable enough to say, "I love you and will be faithful to you and will never leave you," creates intimacy.

There are four major components to intimacy in marriage— spiritual, intellectual, emotional, and physical. The level of intimacy you have in each of those areas will be based on how well you develop each area as you spend your lives together. For the most part, intimacy happens naturally as you spend your lives together and learn more about each other. Some areas require work and compromise.

Spiritual Intimacy

Spiritual intimacy is when there is a deep connection between your spirit and your spouse's spirit. The human spirit is that part of us that is deep within that cannot be touched physically. It's composed of our personal values and beliefs and provides purpose for our lives. It is the core of who we are.

Spiritual intimacy is when that strong awareness of God is within both of you and connects you to each other. You may not express or practice your beliefs the same way, but your level of commitment to God internally is the same. Spiritual intimacy happens when your spiritual values in terms of faith, hope, and love are in agreement. You both seek the same source of divine guidance for daily living and in times of need. Spiritual intimacy is important when times are good and when there are life challenges. When you have spiritual intimacy, it will be the bridge that brings the two of you together when life's challenges try to tear you apart.

Prayer is an effective foundation and tool for building spiritual intimacy. Prayer has always been a huge part of my marriage. There have been times when we had a conflict and neither one of us would give in. Through prayer, God softened our hearts and helped us to identify and resolve the real issues.

When you pray about situations in your marriage, pray objectively for one another. Don't ask God to change him or her. Ask God to show both of you how to show love in this situation. Ask God to reveal the truth to both of you. Ask Him to be the Mediator and to show the two of you how to resolve the issue. After you pray, just step back and watch the situation unfold. Do not take matters into your own hands. Go and live your life, enjoy each day the best you can, and in time, everything will work out. This is something I have learned over the years.

When you take matters into your own hands, you only make the situation worse. Instead of spending time worrying, spying, accusing, blaming, punishing, we should pray for our spouse, talk things over with them like a reasonable adult, and then move forward and allow God to work in us. Always pray for each other—whether you pray together or in private. Always pray about every situation and challenge. Spiritual intimacy is created and gets stronger between the two of you as you pray throughout the years.

Intellectual Intimacy

Intellectual intimacy is when you have a meeting of the minds on topics that interest both of you. Intelligence may have even been something that attracted you to your future spouse.

Intellectual intimacy taps into your mind and connects the two of you on a mental level. You don't have to have the same degree of education to be intellectually intimate. The intimacy comes from seeing something in each other that you connect with. Perhaps you both enjoy reading the same things, discovering the same things, or learning the same things. This is intellectual intimacy. When you're able to have stimulating conversations, this is intellectual intimacy. Some couples fall in love because they are able to have great conversations.

Emotional Intimacy

Emotional intimacy is when you are aware of each other's emotional needs. Emotional needs could be a need to feel secure and that you won't walk out in times of trouble. Some might have a need for constant compliments. Some might need frequent contact throughout the day every day. This is what some people call "work." I've heard people say they never want to get married because they hear it's a lot of work. Maintaining emotional intimacy is probably the work they are referring to. When two people are aware of each other's needs and work to make sure those are met, it creates emotional intimacy.

Emotional intimacy happens when someone you care about loves you and cares about you and respects your feelings and who you are. They're not wishy-washy on whether or not they will stay with you and commit to you. They are fully vested in creating a trusting and committed relationship.

Emotional intimacy happens when there is nothing blocking the emotional connection between the two of you. You'll know you have emotional intimacy when there is a certain peace between you when you communicate with each other. When you talk to each other, your speech will be gentle and respectful. Even in disagreements you will consider each other's feelings. When there is emotional intimacy, you can tell when the other person is happy or sad. With emotional intimacy comes compassion and the ability to empathize with your spouse. Even further than that, emotional intimacy will make you want to protect him/her and look out for their best interest. It will even prompt you to put his/her needs before your own at times.

Physical Intimacy

Physical attraction is often the first sign of a connection between two individuals. There's a physical connection that sparks an interest and good feelings inside. It can start with a flirty look or a smile. Physical intimacy is when there is an expression of love or closeness through touching. The keyword is interaction. If you are giving and not receiving, it's not intimacy. Physical intimacy is a two-way street.

Physical intimacy may or may not involve sex, but it definitely involves touching. Physical intimacy and sex are not one and the same. In physical intimacy, there is a level of warmth, mutual affection, and closeness. In sex, there is physical interaction that may or may not be accompanied by affection. It doesn't take love and affection to have sex, but it does require love and affection to have physical intimacy.

How Physical Intimacy Occurs

Physical intimacy starts way before you enter the bedroom. It starts with emotional intimacy as you make emotional connections with your spouse throughout the day. It could also start with intellectual stimulation with your spouse. Emotional intimacy can happen a number of ways—a flirty text message, a compliment, or saying a heartfelt genuine "I love you." It can also start with more physical interaction like taking a shower together, wearing a sexy outfit, sharing a candlelight dinner, engaging in a passionate kiss, walking and holding hands, or giving a full body massage. Intellectual intimacy can happen through an exciting conversation. Perhaps you and your spouse have had conversations that energized or roused you. Emotional and intellectual intimacy could lead to physical stimulation at times.

Once your minds are stimulated through emotional or intellectual intimacy, your bodies respond. Her mind sends a signal for her body to become lubricated. His mind sends a signal to his body to erect. Now both parties are ready for sexual intercourse.

In physical intimacy, you are sharing yourself and your body with your spouse. One of the most beautiful things about marriage is the physical intimacy. It's amazing how the female and male bodies fit perfectly together. The goal of physical intimacy is satisfaction and enjoyment. When you get married, be prepared to share your body with the one you love. If physical limitations prevent you from being physically intimate with your spouse, there are other ways to show him/her that you love them. If you are physically limited, here are some ways you can show your spouse you love them:

- Kissing them passionately with no inhibitions.

- Spending time with them in the park, romantic restaurant, or other place with nice scenery.

- Giving them a thoughtful greeting card.

- Having a couple's spa day.

- Writing a love letter to them.

Get Rid of Hindrances to Intimacy

In order to have enjoyable physical intimacy, you must get rid of all hindrances in your mind. Physical intimacy fulfillment starts in your mind. Evaluate your mind to determine if you have any mental roadblocks to intimacy. Some roadblocks can be childhood sexual trauma, self-gratification, pornography addiction, promiscuity, fear due to lack of experience or recent experience.

Childhood or Adult Sexual Trauma

No one deserves any type of physical or sexual abuse. There are many people who have experienced sexual abuse at the hands of a horrible aggressor. Memories of abuse can enter your mind and prevent you from trusting yourself emotionally or physically to anyone. It can cause horrible flashbacks in your head. If you have experienced any kind of abuse, molestation, or rape in your past, please know that you did not deserve it. It is not your fault that those horrible things happened to you.

Abuse is something that is hard to remove from your memory bank. It can scar you for life. To be able to have loving and free intimacy with your spouse, it's important to move past any pain and suffering you have experienced. You deserve a lifetime of loving intimacy with your spouse. Conduct an assessment of your thoughts, feelings, and emotions regarding bad physical events in your life. If memories of your past interfere with being able to move into emotional, intellectual, or physical intimacy, consider seeking professional help with moving past the distress. There are licensed professional counselors who can give you tools to help manage the thoughts and memories that keep you from living a fulfilled life with your spouse.

Self-gratification

In order to have true intimacy in your marriage, it's important to move from the autoeroticism of self-gratification to the "we" of lovemaking. Sexual gratification obtained solely through stimulating one's own body is an activity that is common among singles and also married people. When you are used to self-gratification through masturbation, making love with someone sometimes does not give you the same experience. Studies show that many people continue to masturbate after marriage because they grew to prefer that type of stimulation. It also gives them a level of confidence and control that they do not get in making love to someone.

The ideal situation in marriage is to be able to gain sexual pleasure from your spouse and to prefer your spouse over masturbation. Pure sensuality and sexual pleasure between you and your spouse can help create physical intimacy in your relationship. Physical intimacy can give you a sense of closeness and a bond between you and your spouse.

It is an established fact that married people have more sex than singles, perhaps because they have more continuity. Nevertheless, self-gratification often occurs in marriage. Moving from the "me" of self-pleasure to the "we" of lovemaking can be problematic if someone has been single and celibate for a long period of time before getting married.

It may take some time for them to move to the "we" of lovemaking. Sometimes it takes longer to move from self-gratification to the "we" of lovemaking because the couple does not communicate openly about their bodies and what works best for them. Sharing such deeply personal matters is not always easy early in the marriage. Rather than spending time with self-gratification, spend that time getting to know your spouse's body and allow them to get to know yours. Take the time to explore each other together.

Pornography Addiction

Pornography addiction can be a hindrance to physical intimacy with your spouse because it affects your ability to share yourself freely. When someone watches pornography, masturbation usually accompanies. To be able to freely share yourself with your spouse in marriage, you have to let go of pornography. It can hinder your physical relationship with your spouse not only because of it being a secret for you, but also because of its effect on lovemaking. Because masturbation usually accompanies pornography, you are cheating your spouse out of true intimacy because you are satisfying yourself instead of your spouse. Masturbation could also stifle your ability to fully enjoy being with your spouse because you have already satisfied yourself beforehand.

Instead of watching someone else making love in a video, engage yourself with your spouse in your own love-making reality. By not having any secrets of watching pornography, you have a level of openness and honesty in your physical intimacy which in turns strengthens your unity.

Promiscuity

When someone is promiscuous, they feel they just can't seem to be satisfied with one person. There's something in their head that makes them feel they can't settle with just one person. Something inside them draws them to multiple affairs with different people. If you have this type of struggle and you have not been successful at managing it, it's best that you stay single and not get married until you move pass this. If you feel the need to date multiple people at a time and you're not satisfied with just one person, figure out why you have this need. Talk to a licensed professional counselor to get help in identifying the source of this behavior or desire. Consider waiting to get married until after you have resolved the underlying issue that causes the promiscuity. If you are not able to commit to one person, you would be unhappy in marriage and so would your spouse.

Fear Due to Lack of Experience

Maybe abuse, pornography, or promiscuity is not something you have experienced or struggled with. Maybe your concern is that you've been single for so long you're not sure how to approach sharing yourself physically with someone in marriage. The good news is that not having sex for a while enhances your sex life when it does happen. It increases your desire for sexual activity, which could possibly lead to more satisfaction when intercourse begins again. Once you do experience making love, you will experience stronger, longer-lasting gratification.

Perhaps your lack of experience is due to your personal decision to be celibate. People choose celibacy for different reasons. Some of those reasons are:

- Spiritual solitude and commitment

- Promise to themselves to remain a virgin until marriage

- To take a break from sexual relationships to regain emotional or other stability

- Waiting for the right person to come along

Whatever the reason for celibacy, it can be somewhat challenging when you finally are sexually active. Because you've been in a constant state of abstinence, your mind may have trouble transitioning to the freedom of sex. This is especially true if you refrained from sex for spiritual reasons.

When I was single, I attended a singles conference where the speaker said, "Honey, the Lord can freeze it for you so you don't have any temptation." Well, when I heard that, I said to myself, *I don't want it to be frozen. I want to be ready and able to function whenever I do get married.* The question in my mind was: *How do I remain celibate until I get married, but be physically ready for my husband when I do get married?*

The question is: how do you transition from a life of solitude to a life of regular physical intimacy with your spouse?

From Celibacy to Sex

Here are some steps to take to make the transition from celibacy to physical intimacy with your spouse:

1. Realize that sex is not a sin. In fact, it was created by God. When God created woman for man, He created a perfect fit. He designed our bodies to fulfill each other. When the woman is stimulated, it leads to lubrication, and therefore prepares her body for her husband to enter.

2. What you did to remain celibate all those years, you will now do the opposite. Instead of keeping your mind pure from thinking about sex and desiring physical activity, allow your mind to freely think about being physically intimate with your spouse.

   - Sex starts in the mind. Allow your mind to be open to all possibilities in bed with your spouse. Making love is a great way to express your love for your spouse. Think about who you are and what you have to offer your spouse in the form of making love. Think about him or her and what stimulates you physically about them. Focus on the two of you becoming one as you express your love to each other.

3. Tap into your sexuality. Think about what makes you feel sexy. Is it a sexy outfit or lingerie? Then wear a sexy outfit to bring out your sensuality. Does a certain song make you feel sexy? Then play it. Does being naked make you feel sexy? Then take it all off! Feel free to do whatever it is that makes you feel sexy with your spouse, with no inhibitions.

4. Prepare yourself physically to feel sexy. Do Kegel exercises to prepare and strengthen your lower muscles. A Kegel exercise is when you do repetitive contractions of your pelvic floor muscles. This exercise has been proven to improve women and men's sexual function. You can also do push-ups to build your strength and stamina.

5. Don't hold back from making love with your spouse. The more you make love to your spouse, the more you will want to make love to your spouse. Once you get out of the habit of making love, you run the risk of losing interest and you might get used to not having it. Just as you get to know their personality, get to know their body and invite them to get to know yours.

If you're uncomfortable speaking out loud to let your spouse know what you like, or if you simply don't know what you like, try this exercise:

*   Take a few minutes before you make love to touch each other to search for those areas on your body that you enjoy.

*   Lay down on your back, take a deep breath, and relax.

*   Instruct your spouse to slowly rub his/her fingers up and down your entire body.

*   As your spouse moves his/her fingers up and down your body, pay attention to those areas that you enjoy.

*   When your spouse touches an area you enjoy, let him/her know by either groaning softly or just say something like, "I like that."

*   Do this exercise as often as possible until you and he become more and more familiar with your sensuous spots.

6. Physical intimacy should be right after a bath or shower so that you can have a clean, refreshing scent, even with a soft body spray. If there are children in the house, make sure your door is locked and that your kids know the signal for "do not disturb."

7. If you so desire, play romantic music to set the mood for your physical intimacy. Make sure the music is appropriate—not too loud, not too fast, and not music that reminds you of someone or something else. Soft jazz music is a safe and sexy genre if you're not sure what type of music to play.

8. Don't talk too much when you are exploring each other. Try to talk more with your body, hands, lips, tongue, or soft moans and groans.

Remember, you have a lifetime to experiment with each other and get to know each other physically, mentally, and emotionally. Take your time releasing yourself to him/her as you learn how to share yourself with each other.

Don't worry about how often you make love or what position you use. Don't let television or other people define what is a "normal" or "healthy" amount of sex for your marriage. Just enjoy getting to know each other.

Demonstrate Core Values Needed for Lifelong Intimacy

There are certain values that every marriage must have for lifelong intimacy. Although we are all unique and every marriage is different, there are some core qualities that we must have if we want to enjoy our marriage. The goal in marriage should not be to "survive" many years together—the goal should be to "thrive" many years together.

I know so many couples who are merely living together. There is no affection shown in or outside of the home. They don't do any activities together. They barely talk to each other and when they do, there's no affection or passion. It's as if they're living together as roommates. These are not qualities of a thriving marriage.

With certain core qualities, your marriage will have the right foundation to thrive. Think about these qualities and decide if these are attributes that you and your future spouse demonstrate.

Prayer

Don't minimize the power of prayer in your marriage. I know people who changed drastically because their husband or wife prayed for them. I've seen relationships that were on the brink of divorce and turned completely around because of prayer. I can affirm that prayer has been the glue that has kept my marriage together. Fortunately, my husband and I both believe in the power of prayer. We have been in tough situations where our minds were changed regarding the way we thought about certain things that were hurting our relationship. If we didn't believe in prayer, I don't know if some changes would have occurred. There were times when I blamed him for stuff but through prayer, I was able to see where I was the one who was wrong. When you sincerely pray and ask God to help you in your marriage and show you how to show love to each other, God will answer your prayers.

Having a private devotion time has been such a blessing and positive impact on my marriage. Every morning I spend about five minutes praying to God and reading a few Bible verses. Then I play worship music as I get dressed. It's during these times that I'm preparing my heart and spirit for my day. It seems that this time lays the foundation and gives me the strength I need for the day. I always pray for my husband during this time. It helps me to see him as God's child just as I see myself as God's child. Seeing him as God's child prevents me from holding anything against him because I know God takes care of him and disciplines him just like He does me. God is no respecter of persons. He will handle every situation in your lives much better than you can.

Mutual Respect

Emotional intimacy causes you both to care about each other's needs. If you are constantly making sure your needs are met without checking to see if your spouse's needs are met, then your marriage will suffer. No one will ever meet anyone else's needs 100 percent of the time, but the key is to be sincere in looking out for each other. Both of you should constantly check in with your spouse to see how they're feeling emotionally. At the same time, you should not hold back when it comes to expressing your emotional needs when necessary.

In our early years of marriage, my husband and I had to adjust to each other's communicate style. His communication style was more direct, and his tone of voice was a little sterner than I liked. It took some time for him to learn that he needed to "soften" the way he spoke to me in certain situations. In my communication style, I tend to be pretty "long winded" which means I use a lot of words to say something that could be said in much fewer words. In time my husband has gotten used to that. A major adjustment we also had to make was how to communicate in times of conflict. Everybody handles conflict differently. We had to get professional counseling to help with our individual conflict management styles. The counselor gave us some effective tools to use, which eventually became a natural part of our lives.

The common ground in your daily interactions should be mutual respect. Respect the role that you play in each other's life. Respect the sacredness of your marriage in the following areas.

Respectful in Social Interactions

One thing I have noticed in a lot of singles is that there's a time period between engagement and marriage or even early in their marriage when they have to adjust how they interact with people of the opposite sex. There's a certain way that some single people carry themselves that is somewhat flirty, even when it's not their intention. It might be your smile, a hug, or the way you say hello. It's basically the body language when you interact. With me, it was always my smile and the way I look directly in people's eyes when I talk to them. I learned that this can sometimes be considered flirty.

It's perfectly fine to flirt with other singles when you are single. I believe you should present an image of openness to let other singles know you are approachable. However, when you get married, all the flirting should stop. After marriage, your disposition or behavior should say, "I am married and committed to my spouse." After marriage, your body language and flirting should be towards your spouse and not other people.

There's a time period after marriage when we are still in transition with our social interactions. We should be careful with the body language, the smiles, and the hugs to not appear to be flirting. Flirting with others when you are married would be disrespectful not only to your spouse, but also dishonorable to the sacredness of your marriage. Marriage is a sacred union and should be taken seriously and treated with respect. Marriage holds both of your hearts and souls in one vessel and you are to hold that vessel to the highest regard.

Here are some things that could possibly seem like flirting to someone who is not your spouse:

- You're at the grocery store, you see a guy or a lady, and you wink at him/her.

- You carry on a long, overly friendly conversation with someone.

- You greet someone with a tight full-frontal hug.

- You compliment someone on their outfit or hair.

The reason flirting should stop when you are married is because it could not only send the wrong message to the person you are flirting with but can also make your spouse uncomfortable. If your spouse is not present when this flirting happens, you are disrespecting your marriage with this indiscreet behavior.

Flirting doesn't have to end completely when you get married. If you enjoy the excitement of flirting, then shift your flirting to your spouse. Flash that sexy smile at your wife when she enters the room. Whistle at your husband when he puts on a new outfit. Give your husband a big tight hug when he walks in the house. Pat your wife on the behind as she walks pass you. Flirting keeps fun and excitement in your marriage and promotes foreplay for your sex life.

Open Communication

Knowing how to best communicate with each other creates lifelong intimacy in your marriage. Be prepared to let your spouse know how you are feeling and what's on your mind. Some people have a hard time communicating their needs and wants. They would rather hold things in instead of talking about it. Perhaps they feel the other person should already know how they feel. Don't take the chance of someone knowing how you feel. Make sure they know for sure how you feel by telling them and making sure they understand.

Communicate your feelings with your spouse in a loving way. When you communicate, remember that it's not what you say but how you say it. The right message can go across the wrong way depending on how you say it. For true intimacy, be open, honest, and loving in your conversations with your spouse. Start your sentence with something like, "When you do… it makes me feel like…"

Empathy

Empathy is a skill that would prevent a lot of conflict in marriage if more people used it. Empathy is the ability to understand and share another person's feelings. In other words, be willing to put yourself in the other person's shoes before you react. This has helped me in so many situations, especially in the area of forgiveness. When my husband and I have been in tough situations, I ask myself, how would I want him to treat me if I was in his shoes? When I step back from the situation and ask myself this question, I always end up with a different way to respond.

When issues arise in your marriage, address the issues with compassion and emotional support. Work through it with the goal of trying to understand what happened and why. Consider the person's true intent instead of assuming they did it to hurt you or to be deceitful. Maybe they didn't mean any harm at all. Maybe they didn't realize the consequences. Talk to each other openly about it and remind yourself to listen with a compassionate and empathetic heart. Try not to make any condemning comments.

Put all bad feelings and past indiscretions to the side and listen with a fresh and open mind. Listen to what they are saying with no interruptions so that you can get the full picture. Repeat what they said back to them to make sure you understand. Let them know that you appreciate their honesty. Be honest and express to them why their actions hurt you. Ask them if they understand why it hurt you.

Discuss possible ways the two of you can get on the same page to make sure it doesn't happen again. End the conversation by assuring each other of your love, devotion, and commitment to each other. If you're unable to have a productive conversation, you may need to seek professional counseling. Licensed professional counselors can give you tools and techniques to use for conflict resolution in your marriage for years to come.

Trust

Trust is essential in marriage yet with some, it's the hardest thing to do. When there has been a breach of trust in previous relationships or even in your current relationship, it's hard to trust again. When you have opened your heart to someone and loved them without restraint, and then they betray your trust by doing something you never thought they would do, it is heart breaking. It crushes the very spirit you loved them with. You ask yourself, "How could they do this to me?" You try to move forward but it's hard.

As time goes by, the pain of betrayal slowly diminishes but you never forget what they did. Well, if we want to have a productive and thriving marriage, we must forgive the person who betrayed us. I'm not saying we should keep them in our life if they have done irreparable harm and continue to do so. I'm saying that in order to live a physically, mentally, and emotionally healthy life, we have to let go of any hard feelings we have towards those who harmed us. If we don't forgive, our hearts will continue to drag, and we will cheat ourselves out of happiness.

Here are some dictionary definitions of trust:

To offer credit.

Firm belief in the reliability, truth, ability, or strength of someone or something.

Confidence, belief, faith, freedom from suspicion or doubt, sureness, certainty, assurance, reliance.

Marriage requires some level of trust. There should be some hope and expectation for your marriage or otherwise what's the use of being married. Trust is something that is earned.

If you've been hurt before, consider these steps to learn to trust again:

1. See trust as a type of "credit" you are offering your spouse. Give them a clean slate of credit with your open heart, removing all doubt.

2. Remember that the person who hurt you has moved on with their life. It's more likely than not that they are not

even thinking about what they did. Why drag yourself down by rehearsing that memory in your mind when they're not worried about it.

3. Forgiveness is for you. It's not for the other person. If you don't forgive, you are carrying something hard in your heart that could lead to bitterness and even illness. Clear your mind and heart of all thoughts and feelings of unforgiveness.

4. Consider your own slip-ups and how someone forgave you one day. Surely there are mistakes you have made or people you have hurt in the past. Without condemning yourself or feeling ashamed, consider how you have been forgiven and was given a second chance.

Commitment

Single people have the option to stay in a relationship as long as they remain interested in the other person. If their feelings for that person change, they move on to the next person they're interested in. They could also date more than one person at a time if they choose to do so. The rules for singles regarding monogamy are up to each person in the relationship to decide. Sometimes they will be on the same page regarding whether they will exclusively date each other and sometimes they won't.

On the other hand, most married couples want fidelity. They feel fidelity is safer for the relationship in more ways than one. The explicit visuals shown on television and the Internet can increase the temptation to be unfaithful. This along with other enticements can cause married couples to loosen their grip on their sacred vows of fidelity. If that loosening turns into an actual affair, the relationship is never the same afterwards.

Because infidelity is such a disaster to marriages, you should regularly talk about the state of your marriage with your spouse and try to head off anything that could cause stress on your relationship. Do your best not to cheat on your spouse as it can cause permanent damage. There are many reasons why a person becomes a cheating wife or a cheating husband. Also, contrary to popular belief, men are not the only ones who cheat. I once knew a woman who was a nurse and somehow became entangled in an affair with one of the doctors at her job. They worked together a lot of long hours and one thing led to another. She was married to a great man who adored her and would do anything for her. Somehow, she lost the thrill she once had for her husband and had an affair with the doctor.

There is no single reason why people cheat. The best way to explain it is to say that we are all human and sometimes we go against our own will or good intentions.

Here are some ways that infidelity can be prevented:

- Avoid being alone with someone of the opposite sex. Secluding yourself with someone, whether you are sexually attracted to them or not, is dangerous. Research tells us that infidelity at work is becoming commonplace. Make an effort to not have lunch or take breaks with attractive others. When you travel with a co-worker, avoid meeting in hotel rooms. Meet in public instead. Avoid intimate interactions that create a sense of "we-ness" with a co-worker.

- Consider the impact of infidelity before you start. Infidelity is very harmful to marriage. When you cheat on your spouse, you inflict huge emotional damage on him/her. You destroy trust that you might never get back. You also devastate your children, if you have any, and also other family members and friends who love you as a couple.

- Turn to your moral, religious, or spiritual values for strength when you are tempted to philander with someone outside of your marriage.

- Consider the consequences and everything you could possibly lose through your infidelity. Think about everything you have worked so hard for and the possibility of losing it all.

- Talk to your spouse openly and honestly about your struggle. Ask them to treat you as a friend in need while you talk about it and ask them to help you through this trying time.

Transparency

Transitioning into marriage involves preparing to share yourself emotionally with your spouse. This means you now share your innermost thoughts with your spouse. When you are single, you're used to making your own decisions and holding your concerns inside. Unless you have a close friend to talk to, you're not used to sharing your joys or problems with someone on a constant basis. One of the joys of marriage is that you have someone to share everything with.

One of the areas you should prepare for is to be transparent with the person we're married to. In order to have true intimacy with your spouse, it's good to be open about your feelings—good and bad. When there are things in life that upset you, be willing to talk to your future spouse about it. Don't hold those problem areas inside. Sharing your worries and concern with your future spouse will help build the unity between the two of you. Let them know that you are not expecting them to fix it, but you just want to share what is bothering you.

When there are things that bother you about them, let them know in a nice and loving way. Try to create an open stream of communication. Sharing your thoughts, concerns, fears, and even things that make you happy builds trust and strength in your relationship. It builds a level of friendship that you will need during the rough times. Talking to each other during the good times and bad will strengthen your confidence in each other.

Transparency includes honesty. When you are honest with each other it creates trust and emotional intimacy in your marriage. Secrets are an enemy of intimacy. It's hard to be close to someone you keep secrets from because you constantly have to watch what you say and do. Marriage is a place that is safe for you to share your innermost thoughts. Trust your partner to listen to you and be there for you. Make sure you create a safe place for your spouse to be transparent. Do not discuss your marital problem with friends.

Forgiveness

Forgiveness is a huge part of marital success. There will be bumps and bruises in marriage. If you get stuck on the bumps in the road, you won't be able to move forward. I can't imagine that couples who have been married, 30, 40, or 50 years never had any serious problems along the way. I'm pretty sure that in long term marriages, somebody chose to forgive and move on.

Forgiving your spouse will allow you to move on from the action that hurt you and turned you into a victim to becoming a powerful and self-confident person. **Forgiveness proves that you are strong enough to move past the pain and on to a healthier life.** It will take time to completely forgive and you may never forget, but the sting and pain of the heartache will eventually go away. Be a victor of your life and not a victim. Forgive freely so that you can receive the same forgiveness when you need it.

Staying on Track

Sometimes life offers you an unexpected blow to your marriage. This could be due to a fault of yours or your spouse's, or outside influences. Whatever the case, sometimes you need help keeping the intimacy of your relationship on track. There might be times when a problem will hit you so hard, you just don't know how to handle it on your own. Or, you think you know how to handle it, but it's just not working. You might have situations when one person is at fault, but he/she is not willing to concede admitting their wrongdoing. There might be times when problems seriously threaten the peace and harmony in your home. Difficult situations sometimes arise in the marriage, especially in the early years. Some difficult situations that could occur are:

- Physical or emotional infidelity

- Long term job loss by the highest paid worker in the household

- Serious illness

- Death of a close relative

These are all horrible situations that could have a negative impact on your relationship. Whatever the case, the problem has the potential to either weaken or strengthen your relationship. During tough times like this, it would be helpful to see a licensed professional counselor. They are trained to identify the tools and techniques you need to manage your life skills productively. These tools and techniques can help you stay committed during the tough times. If your counselor is focused on divorce, you have the wrong type of counselor. Your counselor's goal should be to help you find the tools necessary to help maintain your marriage.

The counselor acts as a sort of mediator between the two of you and facilitates healthy and effective communication. My husband and I have had professional counseling several times in our marriage. We've had some situations that interfered with our ability to communicate effectively with each other. We needed some help getting the message across to each other in a way we would be able to hear and understand. Sometimes problems can cause you to say things in a way that's hard to understand. And when you say things a certain way or react a certain way, your spouse won't see or hear what you're really trying to say. Counselors have a way of helping you communicate and see each other's side. Professional counseling also helps you understand why you do some of the things you do.

Some people reject counseling because they're concerned about confidentiality, they feel they can handle problems on their own, or because of the stigma associated with counseling. If confidentiality is the hesitation, consider going to a different city for counseling. If that is not feasible for you, go to an area as far away as you can. If you feel you can handle the problem on your own, ask yourself if you really think you would be unbiased in trying to resolve the issues. With professional counseling, you would have someone who is completely objective from both of you. Choose a counselor that neither one of you knows.

As for the stigma of counseling, dismiss that reservation in your mind and think of counseling as in seeing a medical physician. We go to the doctor for our check-ups and when we are sick. It doesn't mean we are weak or insane when we visit the doctor. It means we care about our physical well-being therefore we go and see the medical professional who has trained for years in how to conduct medical prognoses. The same should be for our mental health and the health of our marriage.

As you prepare to move from single to married life, make sure you understand the benefits of attaining professional counseling and that your future spouse does too. If your spouse prefers not to do counseling, then find out if there are other mediation tools that he or she is willing to use.

One tool that a counselor advised my husband and me to use is to do a "check-in" with each other at least once a week. A "check-in" is when we sit down in a quiet setting with no distractions and we ask each other how the other is feeling. We ask questions like, Is there anything bothering you about our relationship? What am I doing great? What do I need to work on? This guidance was very helpful in our relationship and we still do this occasionally. The "check-ins" help to reveal things that probably never would have been revealed on their own.

Below is a list of five benefits couples receive during marital counseling:

1. You learn how to resolve conflict in a healthy manner. In marriage counseling, you learn communication skills that will help you not only listen to your spouse but to also process what your spouse is saying.

2. You will learn how to communicate your needs clearly and openly without resentment or anger.

3. You will learn how to be assertive without being offensive. Both spouses need to be able to talk about their issues without fear of hurting the other spouse. In marriage counseling, you will learn how to do that.

4. You will learn to process and work through unresolved issues. Marriage counseling offers a safe environment for expressing any unhappiness you feel. Getting your feelings out into the open with the help of a trained professional may be all you need. You may find that your spouse is more willing to work together to solve problems in the counseling session than they are at home.

5. You will develop a deeper understanding of who your spouse is and what their needs are. You might also learn more deeply who you are and what your needs are.

Counseling can help you keep your marriage on track when you find a good licensed professional counselor. There's no shame in needing an outside party to get a glimpse of your relationship and work with you to resolve issues. That outside party should always be someone who is educated, experienced and skilled at helping couples build their lives together. The counselor should be someone who is unbiased and who both of you are comfortable with. A good counselor will work with you to try and figure out what the two of you need to do to maintain lifelong intimacy.

Actions to Take to Prepare for Lifelong Intimacy

1. Pray and ask God to show you daily how to speak to each other's heart. Ask God to keep you in unity and to not let anything or anybody tear you apart.

2. Continue to date your spouse after marriage. Continue to give flowers and gifts or whatever you do to impress while you are dating. Give your spouse nice compliments from time to time. Treat them with the same respect and honor you did when you were dating. That also means you keep your appearance nice. Don't wear sweats and t-shirts to bed. Always look and smell your best, especially at bedtime. Flirt with your spouse daily.

3. Keep lines of communication open. Check in with each other from time to time to make sure everything's okay. Ask them if there's anything you can do to make things better between the two of you.

4. Maintain a positive mindset. Don't allow fear, doubt, unforgiveness, or insecurities to take over your mind and cause you to give up on your marriage. Get rid of everything or everybody that have a negative influence on how you feel about your marriage. Assume only the best about your spouse. If there have been problems in your marriage that have been resolved, pray and ask God to help you move forward from that and not rehearse them in your mind. If there are problems that have not been resolved, seek professional help from a licensed unbiased counselor.

5. Maintain your individuality. Your unique personality is what makes your marriage exciting. Revisit the personal statement you wrote in chapter two (step two) and make sure you are staying true to who you are. If you've lost track of your personality, read chapter two again and get back on track. Make sure you keep those things about you that your spouse married.

Scriptures to Read to Prepare for Lifelong Intimacy

Love is patient, love is kind. It does not envy, it does not boast, it is not proud. It does not dishonor others, it is not self-seeking, it is not easily angered, it keeps no record of wrongs. (1 Corinthians 13:4-5)

The Lord God said, "It is not good for the man to be alone. I will make a helper suitable for him. (Genesis 2:18)

Above all, love each other deeply, because love covers over a multitude of sins. (1 Peter 4:8)

Let him kiss me with the kisses of his mouth! For your love is better than wine. (Song of Solomon 1:2)

Let your fountain be blessed, and rejoice in the wife of your youth, a lovely deer, a graceful doe. Let her breasts fill you at all times with delight; be intoxicated always in her love. (Proverbs 5:18-19)

A wife of noble character who can find? She is worth far more than rubies. Her husband has full confidence in her and lacks nothing of value. She brings him good, not harm, all the days of her life. (Proverbs 31:10-12)

But since sexual immorality is occurring, each man should have sexual relations with his own wife, and each woman with her own husband. (1 Corinthians 7:2)

Do not let unwholesome talk come out of your mouths, but only what is helpful for building others up according to their needs, that it may benefit those who listen. (Ephesians 4:29)

Prayer to Pray to Prepare for Lifelong Intimacy

Father God, as I prepare to spend the rest of my life with the person I love, I ask that You teach both of us how to love each other. I pray that You will keep our hearts for only each other. Protect this marriage with Your love. Don't let anything or anyone separate us. Give us unconditional love for each other, in the good times and bad. Help me to trust You as You work in my spouse to be the man or woman of God that You created him/her to be. Fulfill Your love in us and we grow together in spiritual, emotional, intellectual, and physical intimacy. Amen.

♡

Frequently Asked Questions

How do I maintain my current activities and hobbies and include a spouse?

Having a life full of hobbies and activities is actually a great thing to have as a single person. It proves you're not sitting around waiting for someone to help you enjoy life. It's good to be able to participate in activities you enjoy and take care of responsibilities on your own. You might have even met your future spouse at one of your activities.

It takes a lot of work and activities to live from day to day. There are necessities, priorities, chores, and obligations. When there are children, there's soccer practice, dance rehearsals, tutoring, and other activities. There are household chores like laundry, yard work, and dish washing. There are priorities like spending quality time with friends and family. Occasionally there's down time when you can watch a movie or take a nap. We all have our own definition of priorities, leisure, and necessities of life and categorize them differently. What you call a necessity and a priority might be called a nice-to-have by someone else.

I believe it's important to have a full life when you are single. This will decrease the pressure to rely on your spouse for your fulfillment. Marriage should consist of two people joining their lives that are already complete. Your life is complete and his life is complete before you marry. You are content with your life and she is content with hers. Then, when you come together, there's no stress on either one to make the other happy.

To be able to maintain activities and hobbies and also include a spouse you'll have to step back and take a look at all your activities. Think of them in terms of which ones you truly need for self-care or rejuvenation and which ones are taking up time you could use for your spouse. Determine which ones you can continue without sacrificing quality time with your spouse. If you can continue to participate in activities that do not infringe on quality time with your future spouse, there's no need for you to end those activities. If you can do your hobbies and still fulfill responsibilities that are important to your marriage, you can continue your hobbies. The important thing is that you always consider how your activities would impact your marriage.

Cultivating your marriage is very important. It means you are spending quality time together on a regular basis. Quality time means you are interacting with each other without any distractions. The time, energy, love, patience you invest in the marriage is the time, energy, love, and patience you get out of the marriage. Feeding the relationship with quality time is essential to your growth. This is how you will get to know each other. At the same time, it's important to have balance in self-rejuvenation.

I have a friend who visits the hair and nail salon every week. She is also an active participant in her sorority most weekends. Getting her hair and nails done is important to her self-rejuvenation, so when she got married, she continued to do that. She scheduled her visits during times that did not infringe on her and her husband's dinner time together. She also reduced her visits to bi-weekly to accommodate the budget they created to save money. As far as the weekends, it was important to her husband that they spend Saturdays together on weekend trips, so she continued sorority work, but she reduced it to once a month. So, you see she adjusted her hobbies and activities to accommodate the time needed to cultivate her marriage. Her husband also made adjustments to spend quality time with his new bride. He canceled his membership at the country club and started golfing at a local golf course. He also told his buddies he wouldn't be coming to the sports bar anymore. Going to the sports bar meant staying out pretty late and sometimes involved meting female friends. In order to show the utmost respect to their marriage, he decided the sports bar no longer worked for him.

Here are some questions to ask yourself to determine how to balance your activities after marriage:

- *What activities do I have to have to maintain my mental health?*
- *What activities do I participate in that would infringe on quality time with my spouse?*
- *What activities can I ask my spouse to join with me?*
- *What activities do I participate in that could risk the respect I have for my marriage?*

Should I get a prenuptial agreement?

A prenuptial agreement (prenup) is a topic that is related to money, and money is a sensitive topic in a lot of relationships. The purpose of a prenuptial or premarital agreement is to settle financial matters in advance in the event of divorce. Some people consider a prenup an indication that you don't think the marriage will last. Others consider it to be smart financial planning.

If it's your desire or need to feel comfortable moving into marriage knowing you are financially protected should an unexpected separation occurs, then you have that right. The need to feel financially protected has nothing to do with your feelings for your future spouse or expectations for your marriage. A prenuptial agreement is a matter of finances, not a matter of the heart.

If you are comfortable moving into marriage *without* any type of financial protection should an unexpected separation occurs, then you have that right also. Your preference to walk into the marriage with no financial backup plan should separation happen, only means you would rather wait to cross that financial bridge if you were to go in that direction; but for now, you choose not to address it.

Of course, we all hope we never have to cross the bridge of divorce. So, we live our lives full of hope and we work to make our marriage last. Some things to consider in deciding whether to have a prenup are:

- Do you own or expect to own precious heirlooms that you want to make sure stay in your possession should separation occur?

- Do you have or expect to have an abundance of wealth that you want to make sure is distributed fairly?

- Under certain circumstances, prenups can be overwritten in certain states.

Deciding whether to have a prenup should be a decision you make on your own. Then if you decide to get a prenup, you will need to present your decision to your future spouse. This can be a big challenge. Not knowing what his/her response will be is a challenge in itself. If you have decided that a prenup is something you want, be open and honest with your future spouse about it.

If you don't know how to present the idea to your future spouse, I recommend that the two of you meet with a financial advisor to discuss your current and potential finances. The Accountant will gather information from the both of you and help you discover whether a prenup would be in your best interest. This way the pressure is relieved from you to present the idea but is given from a financial expert.

How the two of you handle this sensitive topic will give you a good idea of how your financial conversations will go once you are married. If your future spouse blows up and gets furious at the mention of a prenup, then ask yourself if they're marrying you for money or for love.

How do I manage everything and still make time to date my spouse?

It is important to continue to date your spouse after marriage. Romance should not end after marriage. Romance should continue to go to a deeper level after marriage. Dating your spouse after marriage should be a priority. The good thing about marriage is that you are under the same roof with the person you're married to. This gives you easier access to each other than living apart. This means it's easy to make romantic gestures like leaving sweet notes for each other, wearing sexy lingerie, making breakfast in bed, and bringing flowers home.

In addition to romantic gestures, it's helpful to have a regular date night. When you do, everything else is scheduled around that night. Date night should be protected from all other activities. It is a night that is set aside only for the two of you in order to protect the romance in your life. It's okay to occasionally share date night with other couples, but for the most part, this night should be reserved for just the two of you.

Date night should happen once a week. Usually it is on the weekend, on a Friday or Saturday night, but any day is acceptable as long as it happens on a regular basis. If it ever becomes difficult to have date night on the designated night, it's okay to change it. Date night should not be a chore or an inconvenience. It should be on a night when your minds are free to enjoy each other. If you have children, make sure you have a sitter you trust so that you'll have peace of mind while you're out.

Make a list of all of your activities and prioritize them in order of importance to you. Then decide for yourself which activities you can reprioritize to make room for date night with your spouse.

Do I have to stop hanging out with my single friends?

Good friends are hard to find. If you have friends that are a positive influence in your life, you should maintain those friendships. If you have friends who speak negatively against your spouse, who place you in a mental or physical space you shouldn't be in as a married person, then you don't need those friends.

When you're single and hanging out with single friends, most of the time you're going to places where other singles hang out. And at those places, singles are looking for other singles. A married person should not put themselves in an environment where single people are intentionally seeking out a relationship. I'm referring to places like a singles bar or church singles group.

If you have friends you can openly share with your spouse, you should maintain those. If you have secret friends that your spouse is not aware of, those friendships are probably not appropriate. You should be able to tell your spouse about every friendship you have. Keeping secret friends could cause distrust in your spouse.

Take an honest look at your friends and determine whether they are good or bad for your married life. If you can honestly and openly hang out with your single friends without a negative impact on how you feel about your marriage, then those are friends worth keeping.

How do you establish good habits from the start—respecting each other's quirks, maintaining a Christ-centered relationship, exploring each other's needs and wants?

Establishing good habits from the start will happen naturally as you both accept each other for who you are. One of the exciting things about marriage is finding out each other's habits and quirks. Some things will be fun surprises, and some will be just plain annoying. When you first move in together, you will notice each other's habits and ways of doing things. One likes to sleep with the light on, the other doesn't. One leaves cups on the coffee table, the other puts them in the sink. One likes the toilet tissue roll where the tissues rolls over, the other likes it where it rolls under. One likes to sleep all over the bed, the other likes to sleep on one side and likes to cuddle. One is a "night owl" and likes to stay up late, the other is an "early bird" and likes to go to bed early so they can get up early. One likes to have friends over often to visit, the other doesn't. One likes to keep the house clean, the other likes to leave things laying around. One expresses their every thought, the other is quieter and more reserved. One tells all their personal business to family and friends, the other is very private. These are all differences that can happen in a new marriage. The answer to the question of establishing good habits, respecting quirks, maintaining a Christ-centered relationship, and exploring each other's needs and wants is – constant communication. You have to talk to each other and let each other know how you feel. As you learn each other's habits, quirks, needs, and wants, be open and willing to accept them for who they are. Don't try to change their quirks or habits, but let them know when something seriously bothers you. Address it head on and before it goes on too long and work out a resolution together. Your new marriage will be a process of getting to know each other. Look at the process as a wonderful opportunity to share your life with someone under the same roof. Accept the discovery of their quirks, habits, needs, and wants as pleasant surprises. Focus on the positives and allow them to be themselves so that both of you can be comfortable and enjoy your home together.

How do I know his preferences in the bedroom?

Knowing your future spouse's preferences in the bedroom will come with experience as the two of you explore each other. The key is to have fun while you are exploring. First, get rid of any and all past experiences in your mind. It's very important that you intentionally clear your mind of any sexual experience you have had in the past. If you don't clear your mind, it could have on impact on your marriage. Whether they are good experiences or bad, make every effort to not dwell on those in your mind. If your past involved horrible traumatic sexual violations, steps must be taken to help you in a healing process. Seek assistance from licensed professional counseling to help you along the way.

As you explore each other's preferences, communication is key. You need to let each other know what you like and don't like when you're together. Don't assume that you already know their preferences or that they should know your preferences. Preferences should be communicated either verbally or non-verbally. As you experience intimacy together and you communicate before, during, and after intimacy, you will learn each other's preferences.

Communication *before* intimacy is called foreplay. Foreplay starts *before* you even enter the bedroom. Foreplay can be a pat on the behind, a kiss on the neck, a compliment, a sweet text message or love note, a sexy smile or wink, a kind gesture, a kiss on the ear, a gentle brush against their body when you walk by, saying "I love you," or a kiss on the lips.

Communication *during* intimacy is when you really discover their preferences. Their responses, either verbal or non-verbal will confirm this for you. Likewise, your responses will confirm your preferences for them. Don't be shy about exploring different parts of their body. As you move your hands and try different ways of making love, pay attention to their verbal and non-verbal responses. Also, don't hold back in expressing your pleasure to let him or her know the things you enjoy. The more you communicate during intimacy, the more you will know about each other. Use words like, "How's that?" "Do you like that?" or "Want more?" to hear their preferences. If there's something you don't like, use words like "Not there," "Let's try something else," or gently move their hand to a different part of your body that you do like. The important thing is to enjoy each other. It should be a time of pleasure for both of you.

Communication *after* intimacy is when you celebrate the beautiful time you just spent together. This could include a brief or long cuddle immediately after. Cuddling afterwards makes some people, men and women, feel safe and loved. Communication after intimacy is a great time to "check in" and talk about how both of you feel about the intimacy you just experienced and if there's anything you want to change. The check-in shouldn't be a huge formal conversation. Just use words like "That was really good, how was it for you?" "I love it when you… What did you enjoy most?"

In time, you will learn each other's preferences and will naturally know how to approach each other before, during, and after bedroom intimacy. Just make sure you enjoy the discovery process and that you never allow any intrusions in your bedroom. Your bedroom is your sacred place reserved for only the two of you to consummate the love you have for each other on a regular basis. Your bedroom is the place where you rejuvenate the passion you have for each other as often as possible.

Summary

Successfully and productively moving from single to married life means knowing yourself, who you are marrying, shifting your mindset to marriage, and growing in lifelong intimacy. Always let love be your guiding principle as you walk through each of these steps. In every move you make, during the good times and bad times, through the successes and the struggles, always let love rule. When in doubt, anger, or confusion, always choose love in your response as you merge your lives together as one.

Moving from "me" to "us" means two independent individuals who are already living a fulfilled single life are coming together to form an ever-growing relationship. It's when you bring your whole true self into the marriage and you help each other bring out the best in each other.

Each step of the "Me to Us" process will give you a deeper understanding of your relationship with your future spouse as you grow. But the process doesn't end with step four. The cycle starts all over again with step one where you continue to learn more about yourself. Then you will move to step two again and learn more about your spouse. This is why marriage never gets boring. When you actively participate in each of the steps, growth and excitement are inevitable. As you move through the steps, keep the love for your spouse and commitment to him or her at the heart of everything you do, while at the same time keeping your personality alive.

After marriage, when you find yourself in troubled situations with your spouse and you don't know what to do, ask yourself, "What action could *I* take that would demonstrate my love for *"Us"*? As you move from "me to us", remember the big picture—to present to the world a representation of love and light. Focus on your individual purpose in life and how you can demonstrate that daily in your marriage and in life. Don't let anything keep you from fulfilling that.

Wake up every morning being thankful for another opportunity to enjoy life with your spouse. Forget about what happened yesterday. Make the most of every day.

Love is patient. Love is kind. It does not envy. It does not boast. It is not proud. It does not dishonor others. It is not self-seeking. It is not easily angered. It keeps no record of wrongs. Love does not delight in evil but rejoices with the truth. It always protects, always trusts, always hopes, always perseveres. Love never fails. (1 Corinthians 13:4-8)

Suggested Resources

Here are some resources I have found helpful.

Take Time to Get to Know Yourself

Anita Reed, *Understanding Yourself and Others Personality Profile*

Brenda Bence, *Master the Brand Called You: The Proven Leadership Personal Branding System to Help You Earn More, Do More and Be More at Work*, Global Insights Communications, LLC

Patrick E. Winfield II, *Unleashing Greatness: Learning to Tap Into Your Potential*

Get to Know Your Future Spouse

Madelyn Burley-Allen, *Listening: The Forgotten Skill*, Gildan Media, LLC

John Gray, *Men are from Mars, Women are from Venus: The Classic Guide to Understanding the Opposite Sex*: Quill, An Imprint of HarperCollins Publishers

T. D. Jakes, *He-Motions: Even Strong Men Struggle*, Putnam Adult

Shift Your Mindset for Married Life

T. D. Jakes, *Let It Go: Forgive So You Can Be Given*, Atria Books

Joyce L Rodgers, *Fatal Distractions: Uncover the Roadblocks that Keep you from Fulfilling your Destiny*, Charisma House

Prepare for Lifelong Intimacy

Tony Evans, *Kingdom Man: Every Man's Destiny, Every Woman's Dream*, Focus on the Family

Adam Houge, *If You Change Your Words It Will Transform Your Life*

The Book Conversational Bible, Tyndale House Publishers, Inc.

www.ingramcontent.com/pod-product-compliance
Lightning Source LLC
Chambersburg PA
CBHW030251030426
42336CB00009B/337